We Need a Reckoning

Poetry, essays, and memoir by women and non-binary
poeple of color of the Tacoma, Washington region

Edited by gloria joy kazuko muhammad

We Need a Reckoning
Copyright © 2021 by Blue Cactus Press

Edited by gloria joy kazuko muhammad

Cover art by Paige Pettibon
Cover design & layout by Aliko Weste
Title adapted from "New Year's Eve 2020" by Lydia K. Valentine

ISBN: 9781736820919

This anthology was partially funded by the Tacoma Arts Commission, which supports Tacoma's community by funding local artists and arts organizations, providing technical assistance organizing Tacoma's annual Art at Work month, and oversees the public art program.

Blue Cactus Press and the contributors of this anthology work, rest and reside on traditional territory of the Coast Salish peoples, specifically on land of the Puyallup and Nisqually Tribes. This land was taken under duress via the signing of the Treaty of Medicine Creek in 1854. Since then, it has not been returned to the peoples it belongs to.

Here, we acknowledge that we benefit and profit from our existence in the South Puget Sound on Puyallup and Nisqually land. We respect and honor these peoples and the land. We also understand this acknowledgement does not replace the work of building relationships or trust. It is merely the first step on the path to doing so.

Here, we give thanks. We raise our hands.

As women and femmes of color, we carry stories of rejoice, of grief, of resilience, of defeat – stories that sit like markers on our bones so as we age, we carry them with us – stories that pulsate through our blood so that when we finally cross over, we would have already planted legacies in the tiny heartbeats of the next generations to come. It is no small feat, the first day we choose to begin telling our stories. These are holy days.

And yet, more often the not, the world would tell us otherwise. That our words, our stories, our voices should live at a whisper. Are not drenched in the sacred, when in fact, are the sacred. They are the sinews that hold communities together, and when bound are unshakeable.

The təqʷuʔbəʔ (Tacoma) region has its fair share of matriarchs, brimming with words and demanding to be heard, who have finally found a home within the pages of this Women of Color Anthology. A place where we can be us, unsolicited by media who look to purely extract our narratives for clout. We are the heartbeat of this city. The heartbeat of THIS city.

So when you read these pages, and place your hand upon your heart, you'll feel us.

Brandi Douglas,
Puyallup Tribal Member, owner of Multifaceted Matriarch (digital decolonizing consulting), and co-owner of both American Indian Republic (digital media company) and Bella & Belle (creative design studio)

The doors kept closing. I applied here, interviewed there, but nothing.

I'd always been too loud, too blunt, too round, too strong, too smart ... or maybe just not the right kind of smart. I was always too much of everything but not enough of something.

There was and is a raw unease in knowing that while I was born here, the color of my skin and my native language told on me: that I was a different version of "American." Yet, my family's country of origin did not claim me either. So, who am I? An American who doesn't belong? An English speaker who hides their second language? An immigrant's daughter who consistently overachieves to prove her worth, yet is still found unworthy, not quite enough?

This song of not belonging and having no home became old and worn out. The record started to skip from being listened to so many times. Then once, when it skipped, I threw it away and wondered why I'd listened to it for so long. It had brought me comfort; it had provided companionship. At times, this record – with the same lonely songs – had been my only friend.

The song served its purpose. It kept me warm on many nights, protected me through many harsh winters.

When I moved to Tacoma, I realized I'd been carrying around that broken, scratched record that I didn't need anymore. Tacoma felt like home. The people here felt like summer. I was home.

So, when I am asked, *how did you conceive of, imagine, and found the Tacoma Women of Color Collective?* I don't think of words as I much as I just am overcome with emotion: those old feelings of loneliness, of squeezing into tight spaces; the sick feeling of not being heard, like I'm standing at the bottom of an empty well screaming for someone to hear me.

I have grown tired of those feelings. And I found that my gut was right: there are so many other Black, Indigenous and Women of Color (BIWOC) who feel the same way. And they are here, willing and ready to ride into battle with me. To hold our lives with the most tender of hands.

This collection of stories is an ode to these beautiful beings, these moments, these overwhelming seconds of joy and sadness. It's an ode to our experiences. It's an ode to us.

Krista Perez
Founder of the Tacoma Women of Color Collective

Contents

Water

Sky

Breath

Contributor Bios

Editor's Note by gloria joy kazuko muhammad
Publisher's Note by Christina Vega

Wind

El Tiempo de Los Vientos

Cervantes Gutierrez

veo
plumas verdes, rojas y amarillas
          moviendose
Escuchando
          el sonido del agua
Sonido de la vida.
Las abejas volando,
equilibrando la naturaleza.

Y así vamos nosotros
Luchando
por equilibrar el mundo

I see
Green feathers, red and yellow ones
Moving
Listening
To the sound of water,
Sound of life.
And the bees flying,
Balancing nature.

And that's how we are moving,
Fighting to balance the world.

Words

Eileen Jimenez

i find myself looking for home
in water,
in Land,
in touch,
in laughter,
in taste,
in art,
in books,
and in words.
always
always in words.
i'm obsessed with learning words.
i've scoured Spanish, Polish, Latin, Turkish, Russian, French, Japanese
and English for words. always searching for words that embody who i
am
always searching for more than the words i have,
more than the words that have been given to me.
more than the words I've been left for.
more than the words I have left others with.

and yet,
i always come back
back to the beginning
back to simplicity
back to overflowing
back to rupture
back to pain

malcreada
guarded
maleducada
complicated
sobresaliente
abrasive

i want the words that hold me to be
more than my name
more than my degrees
more than my accomplishments
more than my abilities
more than my skin color

more than my hair
more than my body
more of my laughter
more of my soul
more of my brilliance
more.
more.
more.

How to Build a Couplet

Christina Vega

The narrative begins by giving up your body.
Sit down & build a bridge of words from your belly to your wrist.

Chew the corners off.
This isn't about precision, it's about taste.

I'm telling you the truth.
You must call the raccoons up from under the porch.
Let them witness your worship.

The next night & every night thereafter,
try to wake in the corner of the room.

Look sideways. Drag yourself to the letterbox.
Let your hands claw like a bone knife.
This is communion.

Sleepwalker, listen,
this is how you build a couplet:

Let each line consume you.
Become a ghost.
Collect grass clippings.
Choke on grammar & spit it out behind the house.

Make sure to never show your teeth
when the owl comes looking.

Only then will it carry your message
out & into the night.

tejolote

Eileen Jimenez

my hands grip the tejolote of my grandmother's molcajete.
the same way I imagine my grandmother did, her mother before her, her
mother's mother before her, and every Otomi matriarch in my lineage
since time immemorial.

no one taught me how to do this, but my hands are experts somehow. I
watch them move, in a sort of trance. the same way I watched my mother's
hands move on the days she wasn't too tired, on the most special days.

deep inside this hypnotic state, I remember finding safety in my mother's
hums. the hums, that smothered the pain and fear in our home as they
escaped her body, full of joy. her heart elated and full from the bounty
she was providing.

I feel the most like myself in this deep trance, in the sounds of the stones
grinding, in the feeling of my skin against the stone. in the fire of
anticipation in my belly and in my tongue. in the Roberto Carlos, or Julio
Iglesias lyrics that still flood my mind. I feel the most like myself when my
mind slows down and my hands do what they know to do.

I look down at my hands and realize that my hands are not my mother's.
my hands are not tired. my hands are not cracked from picking strawberries
in 100-degree heat. my hands exist in safety. my hands can do this any time
they want. my hands are free to choose. my hands have already chosen. my
hands belong to me. my hands are mine.

and yet, still, I wonder if in these moments, the trance is really spirit, a
guardian, a teacher. somehow two pieces of old, heavy, gray stone have
made my hands feel sacred and my heart feel full.

Palaver

Gaian Bird

My mother sits with me in a place
Where light is clear golden
And warm without heat
It is a place of soft fire
A proving ground
A place of tempering
Here we clean
And dress the wounds of time
                    Dream Time

What is a memoir? Embedded in the word is memory, and memory is always subjective. My memories come unasked for and often at the oddest times. It's hard to call them up at will, yet a memory sharp and hard as fresh ice will pierce the surface of my conscious mind when I least expect or want it. Jessica Dukes, in her article for Celadon Books writes "... a memoir is an intimate look at a moment in time." As a Black Indigenous Womxn, my memories are windows in time and sometimes they become doors in time to step through. Once through them, there are places to pause and sit with the past, listen to the voices of the womxn who made me and shaped my life before I chose a body. A memoir, for me, is more of an intimate *listening* to the voices in my past. Most of my memories have other people in them. It has helped me to seek answers to my own life by being present to their side of things, to see events and time through their eyes more than my own.

There was so much that I shut away because I was not ready to look through their eyes. My own path had not opened enough for me to stand in that force without shrinking from its truth. My generational story and my memories are filled with spilled blood, murdered dreams, a people stolen and subjugated, and a people all but vaporized through genocide. My generational story is also filled with the sacred--the medicine makers, the artists, the story keepers, the healers and the warriors. I've come to know them through the voices of the beloved dead who have sat on my shoulders and kept me upright and breathing until I could heal enough to hear and keep their stories. It is my task, among many, to know their stories through their voices.

A part of my journey of Ancestral Healing and Recovery has been to learn to listen to the voices of the womxn in my family line. I am the last of them. I have dreamed of my mother often since she crossed over in 1978. The dreams were not so much an interaction as me simply seeing her; her body in motion like an Amazon Warrior, her face laughing or angry. I have dreamed my mother rolling out biscuits or hanging laundry in our overgrown backyard on Noble Street. I have even dreamed her calling my childhood name at sunset when it was time to come inside from a long summer day; she would draw out the sounds like the ending of a song. We have never spoken to each other in those dreams. I could only watch her and let the feelings of missing her run their course through me.

About a year ago, I began to dream of returning to my hometown and my old house by flying on the back of a raven. I would enter the house and walk through the darkened rooms. Then I would fly to a place where my mother would be waiting for me and we would simply sit together. I've come to know this place of "soft fire" as a space in dream-time where the living and the dead might commune. It is a place of memory and our conventional marking of time has no meaning. It is a place suspended in an Indigenous knowing between everything we think we understand and everything else we cannot grasp or explain. There are names for it, but what we call it is less important than allowing for it to be a part of how we can choose to move through our lives. The more I open to it, the more peace I find and the more the world makes sense to me.

I invite you to sit with me in the soft fire of my family's palaver. We have gathered, my mother who was Frances, her sister who was my Aunt Rena, and me, the Daughter. We are the dead and the living who come together to sort through the generations of our memories and thread them together.

A portion of our generational story evolved in Delaware, Ohio. Our hometown had been a busy hub on the Underground Railroad. There are houses there still standing today that were safe houses, places where the Light Bearer channeled refugees headed to wherever the death houses from which they came were not. My grandmother Grace came from the enslaved Black folx who stayed and made homes in the small towns and farm land near the Olentangy River. My grandfather Jackson was Black and Cherokee; his grandmother was a Cherokee Freed Woman from the Dawes Rolls who somehow managed to try walking away from the death march to Oklahoma. Ohio was as far as she got and her descendants including my grandfather made the place their home. My grandfather was a Black Indigenous man who was a porter and a nightwatchman. He owned his own home and the land it was on. My grandmother did not have to work and she could stay at home with her girls; grow them up into beautiful flowers. My mother and her sister were gifted Black creatives; my mother was a word wizard, a voracious reader, and a deep thinker. Her sister was a weaver of spells with music and a piano. As I craft this image of my beloved dead, I am shaken by how unattainable these simple creature comforts of home, life and joy were and still are for most Black people. My grandfather Jackson and my grandmother, Grace, had chipped away their own meager pieces of an impossible pie. They created places of light that certainly made them mandatory targets marked for destruction by whiteness. Delaware was a place where white abolitionists had helped us and at the same time exacted the cost of that help through less overt, yet no less violent ways.

FRANCES SPEAKS

Daughter was about six years old when I first seen it. At first, I thought it was what Rena came back with from Cuyahoga County. I tried to tell her not to go up there, tried to tell her that damned Buford was no good, but you can't tell love nothing. I know that now 'cause here I am up in this shack of a house with these four kids and Frank done drank up the 'lectric and water bill money. Hasn't been home since Friday when he got off work. Now this. The others, they get on my nerves so bad I don't know what to do sometimes, but that Daughter is just like her. Always acting strange. Always up in grown folk's business, always stealing her daddy's change off the buffet. Always off by herself or askin' for somethin' she can't have. She wants a piano or a bike or a bride doll or she say she want to be a ballerina. Lord, she makes me so tired just like Rena did...wanting so much there was no room for anything or anybody else to be.

DAUGHTER SPEAKS

Mama's saying it again. I don't know what it means except I feel her so mad she shakes. Sounds like she's crying, but her eyes are dry. I know it must be something awful and I don't want to be that thing she's calling me. Feeble Minded. I asked her once what it meant. She said it meant men would come and take me to a hospital at the state and put me in a coat. My brother would say it when I wouldn't do what he wanted. I'm older than him, but he's stronger and it's hard to get out from under him, but I'm smarter at staying out of his reach. Not Daddy, though. There's no place to hide when I'm already in bed. There's always dimes in his change pile and I take them. Only one at a time. The candy I get from the store around the corner makes my teeth hurt, but I don't care.

RENA SPEAKS

Somethin' about "Stormy Weather", that melancholy kinda minor key...such a longing in them notes. I could ride that river tears and all, no salt, just the sweet sad of my fingers on the keys. They had a decent piano at the joint we were playing the night I seen Payne. I was thinking that it must not have been too long since it had been tuned, prob'ly 'cause it was a pianola. The place wasn't big, but they did have that. When Sim an'em asked me to play with 'em I jumped on it. Wanda over at Holy Tried Stone had been askin' for me to play at church and I just couldn't be bothered with all that. All them hypocrite saints singin' on Sunday and sinnin' the rest of the week... shit. But me and music, oh together we felt all the colors and saw everything good and fine and worthwhile. Me and music we was right together, everything in order and in place. Like wings folding in closed and spreading out wide. That night it was me and "Stormy Weather" when I looked up and seen Buford leaning on the door jamb like he wasn't never scared of anything in his whole life. Like he had just stepped out of a beautiful story and had come there only for me.

FRANCES SPEAKS
It wasn't always like that with Rena. She used to let me come with her sometimes when her and Sim's band would practice. Sim would tease me about always having a book to read. Rena would tell them I was smarter than all of them and to leave me be. She could play anything on the piano. She could hear a song once and play it with her own style. Make you laugh or cry with her playing. Everybody loved her because she was the sweet one between the two of us. I was a moody child. Daddy had been gone for about three years maybe when she come back from Cuyahoga. Buford had gone off with somebody else and them white folks she was working for let her go 'cause she was too sick to work. I tried to tell her nothin' good could come of bein' with a pretty man. Buford was one of them. They don't ever stay with one woman. I thought she was just lovesick over that worthless-ass man. She never did get right though. Just kept sliding further away. Mother was working up at Miz Stratford's doing all the cooking for their family. I had to clean the house, cook, and take care of Rena. I had to keep her clean, fed and out of trouble. She couldn't see good anymore and her right arm was all messed up. Wasn't no doctor for us. I couldn't never rest. It was all on me. Turn my back and the next thing she was over on South Liberty out in the middle of the street staring up at the sky. Somebody was always quick to come tell me to go get her, but nobody wanted to touch her or do nothing for her 'cause they didn't want to get what she had. They called it the bad blood. I thought Rena had got it from Buford. Anyway, she was always up in the clouds someplace or talkin' outrageous about what she wanted and could do. She really believed she just didn't have to follow the same rules other Black folx had to follow. Always wanting what she couldn't have. Now this girl, this Daughter...wearing me out with her wanting and her moods and her secrets.

DAUGHTER SPEAKS
There was that time a long time ago when Mama let me play with an old pocketbook she didn't want anymore. It was my lady bag. It had long straps and it smelled of old leather inside. It made a song through the air when I swung it high around my head. I pretended to be a dancer and twirled around and around until I was dizzy and fell. Mama came in and grabbed my lady bag. She reached for her glasses on the table, but they weren't there. She said, "Where are my glasses?" I just stared at her, watching.

"What'd you do with them?" The belt buckle jingled like a tiny bell. At first it hurt, and I cried and then it didn't, and I floated. I heard voices then I smelled witch hazel. Mama was saying, "She...but she..." I wanted so bad for Mama to love me. Seemed like everything I said or did made her mad or cry or both. She never used the belt after that time, but there were switches and open-handed slaps in my face. Most of the time I could figure out how not to make her mad, but it was trickier to find ways to get her to be nice to me. She told me she was smart in school, so I was too and that helped, but it didn't feel like it was enough. I learned to be kind of satisfied with her not being mad.

RENA SPEAKS

Daughter, you have to understand how it was for us then. Frances was the baby of the family, but she never was babied, you know? She was always the one to take care of things when Daddy was killed. She didn't mean to be so hard. I got away for a while and it was good for a while. Buford and me, well, I think he loved me, but he loved chasing and catching more. It was his nature 'cause he was so pretty, and some women just were drawn in like that. I mean, who don't love beauty? When I got sick, I knew it was Buford that brought it to me. I never wanted nobody but him. I gave up my music for him, went to work for them white folks doing their dirty sheets for him. For a while, he was my music. When I got too sick to keep working wasn't no place else to go but back home. Buford had already left with somebody else, see? And my music was gone. I thought if I came home maybe I could find it again. When I got home, Frances was all I had. Our mother had to go work up at Miz Stratford's and Frances had to do everything for us on her own. I think it broke something in her. When I died, I think she felt relieved and guilty and sad all at once. She didn't know what to do with them feelings. They ate her up from the inside. Folks shunned us because I had the bad blood, but mostly because they felt like Mother acted too good for them, you know? We had a house and most folks didn't. Almost everybody had to work, but Mother didn't until Daddy was gone. Then when Mother died, the white people came and took our house. Mother held on to it as long as she could, but they got it in the end. The worst part was that the neighborhood folks came the day before the sheriff come to board it up and took all of our things, furniture, dishes, everything they could carry. Frances got real lost after that. Everything soft just emptied out of her.

DAUGHTER SPEAKS

I was 18 when I left home for the last time. Mama and I were oil and water. We fought all the time. She kept telling me I would be ruined if I left home and that I would be just like you, Auntie. At first, I didn't understand what she meant about being ruined. I figured out that she was really talking about getting caught up and having a baby without a husband like she did. I still had to leave, though. Oh, I went back here and there but only for a month or two. I kept thinking that maybe Daddy wouldn't bother me, but he always tried. I never told Mama. I was afraid she really would try to put me away in a crazy house. I don't know why I thought leaving would fix me. I just couldn't seem to find my feet, let alone know where they were walking. I was barely aware of breathing in and out. I came to know what out of body really means. It's not an awesome and wondrous experience. It feels like ghosts whispering and you covering your ears. It's last call at two a.m. And slivered light in the morning. Light that promises to wash you clean from careless hands and stale breath on your body. It's sticky thighs and strange beds. It's walk home across town. It's shower and wait tables or clean toilets for rent and wine. Rinse. Repeat. I didn't want to hear the ghosts that were always talking. I didn't want to know what they know. I didn't want to hear them. I didn't want to hear you, Rena and Mama.

FRANCES SPEAKS

It wasn't because I didn't love you. I never tasted goodness after Rena left and they killed Daddy. They said it was a motorcycle accident, but them white men he left with that night came in a truck. I never saw a motorcycle. The white doctor wouldn't examine his body and Mother wouldn't let me see him. I knew those men had done something to him, but Delaware wasn't a place for asking questions and speaking up. It wasn't a place for trying to have more than white folks thought you should have. Daddy and Rena was cut from that cloth—proud, no limits, bigger than life. I saw Rena in you when they put you in my arms. So much life like so many stars in the sky. I thought she maybe had come back to me. I didn't care about Buford, really. I just didn't want her to leave me. We was sisters. Our lives were better with each other. She taught me happy. She took all of that with her when she left and I couldn't find it without her to show me. Maybe if she had stayed, I could have learned to find it on my own. When you were born, I loved you so much it scared me to death. I didn't know how to keep you safe. Rena had a wilderness in her. When I saw her in you, I had to do something so I wouldn't lose you like I did her. She left here so horrible, all of her wrung out and twisted so tight I just knew wasn't nothing left of her inside. I wanted to keep you safe. I wanted you to be alright. I never wanted anyone to hurt you like they did my Rena. It was never for want of love that I hurt you, Daughter.

RENA AND FRANCES SPEAK

Daughter, we been right here with you. We been trying to get through for a long time. You're learning that our story is full of wounds. The ones done to us and the ones we did to each other because it was all we knew. See, you learn from pain and you learn from pleasure. Sometimes, there is no way to tell the difference between them. Sometimes it's easy to mistake one for th'other. Sometimes it's *both and*. You are here with us now in the *both and* of our Palaver. There is pain here and there is healing. The soft fire of our Dream Time gives us eyes to see all sides and all roads. You have our names for a reason--to keep us going--me, her, and now you. We are the healers, the seers; we are the makers and the builders. We are the peace bringers and the holders of space. Your mama and me, we had to be so that you could come. We stumbled and fell down and you have been picking up our missed steps. We have always needed you to be here now. You heal our wounds. You break our chains. You tear apart the whips. You straighten our backs. You give us shape and form. As you have found wholeness, we become whole. In you lives Rena's music and desire. In you lives Frances' heart and fire. You are our people. All of them from forest to mountain to desert to plains and the way into the seas. We live in you and you in us. Because our bodies were not our own, you must claim yours. Because our minds were not our own, you must govern yours. Because we could not rest, you must claim the right to your own.

DAUGHTER SPEAKS

I stop running
Uncover my ears
I descend
Eat the fruit of the dead
Emerge to tell the story
To be sacred is to be afraid
And to walk on anyway
Every day a choice to breathe
Every breath an Ancestor healed
Miracle made flesh
Flesh into Spirit transforming
I am from timeless stretch
Of warriors who protected
Seers who connected
Healers who soothed
Builders who moved
Many mountains
To bring me here
Now
This is my birthright
To be Black, Womxn, and Sacred
I am my Mothers' Daughter

Mama, I go to therapy once a week

Phebe Brako-Owusu

Mama, I go to therapy once a week
Because there's things I want to talk about, and I worry you may not
understand. I know you've seen the news and I know you're worried about
me. I'm hundreds of miles away from Minneapolis, Louisville and
Brunswick but I'm no safer where I am. America is not the country I
thought it would be. I worry for people who look like me. I cry for my sons,
for my husband, who by the way, was told he didn't belong in a town where
he had stopped to buy gas for his government vehicle. He was in full
military uniform. I'm afraid of the cops being called on me, on us.
Sometimes I want to come back home but I'm afraid I will look like a failure
or that I won't fit in the way I used to. I talk to my therapist about this and I
know she's trying, but sometimes I feel she doesn't get it.

Mama, I go to therapy once a week because it feels like it's one of the very
few places I am actually safe. But I'm not getting too comfortable with that
either because no one knows these days.

Mama, I go to therapy once a week just to talk because sometimes it feels
like no one is listening.

Mama I go to therapy once a week
Because there's things I want to talk about, and I worry you may not
understand.

My son just turned 2 and in addition to praying a birthday blessing for him
I found myself praying to God and begging him to not let my son become a
hashtag because he's been hurt or murdered because of the color of his skin.
I pray for God's will to be done but I'm also bargaining for my son's life and
asking for God to give me the wisdom to teach my son how to love himself,
all of himself, and to love others for who they are.

Mama I go to therapy once a week because I'm afraid of that one mo
ment when I will lose it because someone has messed with my son. I go
to process that moment when he moves from being "cute" to becoming a
"threat" because he's Black.

Mama, I go to therapy once a week just to talk because sometimes it feels
like no one is listening.

Signed, an immigrant in therapy

Goodbye

Isha Hussein

If I knew I was going to lose my best friend, I would have spent all the time I could with her.

> *Goodbye, it's time to say it one last time.*
> Your dark brown eyes are like angels dancing in the sky.
> Your smile is like the stars at midnight shining bright.
> *Goodbye, it's time to say it one last time.*

You're the person that gave me life.
Don't know why it's time to say goodbye.
Just want to say bye one last time.

> *Goodbye it's time to say it one last time.*

> I keep saying it wasn't your time to go.

> Still remember when the doctors said
> you were going to be okay
> even though you had health problems.

Now that you're gone, I feel alone.
I blamed the world.
But now I blame myself.

> Your soul flies up to the sky with two angels
> standing by your side.
> I see your figure with my eyes disappearing through
> clouds shades dark and wide.
> Will you make it through the gates of heaven or fall
> through everything bad and full of hate?

Present your sins to Mr. Heaven himself, he loves you like everyone else.
Getting ready to walk through the gates,
Placing your feet past the line.
Happiness overcame your body looking at your daughter below.

Now I'm seventeen years old sitting here feeling alone.
A black hole in my heart that gets bigger and bigger as time goes by.
Goodbye, it's time to say it one last time.

Wishing you were still here,
mom.
Mom, you're my guardian
angel shining bright,
wishing you were here to see the person I
became.

Goodbye, it's time to say it one last time.

Your voice, like roses in a garden.
Giving me hope.
To cope with losing you.
Goodbye, it's time to say it one last time.

Even though I lost my biological mom, I still gained one that loves me just
as much.

Samurai Mom

Marissa Harrison

"Your nose is flat. It looks like this."
And the cherub-faced girl presses her nose against her face
With her index finger.
My friend laughs.
My friend says and does the same.
"You're ugly," they say. "Like a monkey," they say.
I am only five, and now I believe there's something wrong with
How I'm made
I'm the color of waste. The color of mud.
A color that makes them point
A putrid color that
Shows me the contrast of their pale, slinky hair
That moves in the wind.
My hair doesn't move in the wind.
Like the wind I run, my ashy knees bearing the
Burden of bringing me home across the wide and empty cul-de-sac
And there in the doorway of my childhood home
Is my mother. She is more yellow than me
More beautiful than me
More Samurai than me, so much so that I forget her nose
Is flat too
Like mine. Her yellow skin is black like mine.
The girls come to our door.
"Can she come out and play?"
My mother is a lion and her black mane trembles.
"No. She will not play with you again.
 Not if you speak to her like that again."
And then she says, as I hide in the line of the
Warped, tortoise shell window,
With light pouring through, warming my cheekbones
high and yellow,
"You will not speak to her like that again."
My mother talks in that shrill voice I hate.
But I do not hear.
Because today it's not for me
Because today it's only for me
I watch my former friend turn red,
The skin she said was better
Is now colored like mine, and she slowly
Slinks away.
The other girl stays and I respect her for this

For I know the lion's claws
Have heard the deafening roar as it shook
My bedroom walls and rattled the green, blue, purple, yellow
And red hearts
That lived on my white bedspread.
I've even roared in return as her cub, tore and scraped
And fought because that's what she taught me.
But today I have no roar
Because today they stole it from me.
The house is silent now and the lion has gone.
For now she is a tabby cat, and she wraps her body
Coils her striped tail around me and
Scratches my face with her kiss.

I prayed a prayer to my lift my spirit and

Jasmine Hernandez

My angel said to me:

Shouldn't we rejoice in all the chances we get
To grow and grow again
Flowers bloom without being told
And hold no shame in the process

If I can encourage you in any way
It's to use your gifts in your upcoming days
To do the work you were called for, Mija

Step into your mornings without mourning the past
And do not call yesterday a mistake
Please do not carry that weight
Look to the flowers
How they bloom without being told and
Do not apologize for how tall they get
Or how bright, how vibrant or
For how many blooms
They might inspire

That's it
For you, that's what my soul desires

    — Juanita

Call me

Jami Williams

Yesterday, I met my Grandmother
Her name is Cedar
Standing in tall distant memory
Our braided quilt
Speaks of me
Adopting traditions never taught
Living in the lines
Of fingertips
Miniscule matchstick
To light
The face of her
Overgrown wisdom
Adorn my chest with
Bundles of
Cowrie shells instead
Found along a shore
You have never seen
Monsoon purple
Clouds of blood
Upon flesh
Named niizh manidoowag
Instead
Sacred Cedar oil on
A newborn face
Miigwech
From your sapling

Soil

Apparition

Brandi Douglas

Indigenous People's Day.

National Native American Heritage Month.

Native American Heritage Day.

The 'I' in BIPOC, should you still wonder what it means.

What is the value of my existence, when my visibility is contained to specific, succinct periods of time?

To a single letter.

Do I even exist outside the parameters of these 'moments of commemoration?' When does one move from celebrated to seen?

From a letter to a being.

Are we not deserving of 365 days, when we've been answering to roll call with 'here since time immemorial...'

And you still...can't seem to hear us.

Still can't seem to see us.

It's National Native American Heritage month,
but my inscription on this land surpasses calendared calculations of celebration dictated by a Nation who still doesn't get that 'Something Else' is a people who covet unlimited spiritual wealth.

So here's to the days and the month – where we momentarily escape being apparitions.

Here one moment.

Gone the next.

black don't crack
gloria joy kazuko muhammad

>>> *doesn't exist for us*
>>> *with atopic dermatitis*

> my skin cracks, weeps, bleeds

> taking socks off is like Velcro
> showers burn like hand to stove

>>> my scalp sheds snowflakes
>>> in the middle of July

>>>> shaving is a no no

>>>> in case infection occurs

>>> creating a party of staph

>>> *and* then you'll be hospitalized
> *and* not be able to bathe yourself

cortisone will become your state farm

> you look like a fire victim
> is what they will say

>>>> keeping gloves on at night is like
>>>> trying to keep a golden doodle still

> short nails are a necessity

when you go swimming
chlorine will burn

> you'll have to wash your hair again
> as the flakes dance like September

layer your skin with Aquaphor
wrap your feet in saran wrap
& then put your socks on

at home, attain a cold bucket of water
so removal of said socks will be a little easier

your back, you shall cherish
atopic home girl is afraid of your spine

Amy's Pizzas will get old
& you will desperately miss mac and cheese

nutritional yeast will become your sidekick
and oat milk is your friendly neighbor

rice flour will be bland. your cookies will fail.
sorbet is a luxury. you will have an entire pint on your birthday.

the acupuncturist will burn you. you will forgive him.
the homeopathist will constantly exclaim, *quantum healing!*
the naturopath will make you cry when she retires

you'll be tired and exhausted
but you'll also be brave

for weathering the storm
for making flatbread from lentils
for wearing short sleeves during summer

mostly, you will cry when you hear stories

your ears will be one to listen
your smile will be one to laugh until abdomen shakes

for you have tasted fire and walked through flames

yes, black does crack. but the soul never
does.

vocabulary

Katharine Threat

i have not been to many places
beyond where the roots of my family linger
linger is not the right word,
what do you call a home that
at once is yours and not yours at all? what
do you call a place where women gave
birth, again and again,
to children who could not know them
and could not love them,
what do you call a place
where the hatred that this country is
founded on
conflates into a single person?
is person the right word
for a symbol of love and hatred
if that symbol can walk and love and cry but
must do so alone?
country is not the right word either,
for places like this,
where bloodshed is law
and reason is a white man's knuckle dug
into the flesh of anything
he is afraid of?

Vote or Die

Jami Williams

They think the disaster
is the man in the
Big House
that we built
a country built
under beloved,
seething
bloody
chokecherry trees

coming to ask
when we will give it
a rest
as they laugh
and confess an
appetite for rotting
flesh, the way strange fruit
swings from
the family trees
they don't think the disaster

starts and ends
with their existence
and persistence to be pure
to be swaddled in comfort
despite cradling ignorance
my Blackness
holds blood at the root
nothing to gain
inside a white, suppressed
voting booth

a scorched cross
resemblance
of your intentions
the world is already
ending
without your ballot
gaslight
who is capitalism cratering?
can't be white man on the moon,
voting for
racist honky
one or two?

to the confederate ancestors

Katharine Threat

to the confederate ancestors who shall remain nameless and, due to
the laws of history and legacy, disappear

not all racists / years ago / benefit of the doubt / forgiveness / of the time
/ allied / associated / united / adjective; joined by agreement or treaty /
reckon with the fact / blood that nourished / flourished to get here / now
/ may kill you / kill to own you / kill to rape you and sell your children / in
a heartbeat... / but times change / right / associate / partner / accomplice /
collaborator / colleague / noun; a person one works with / do I bother / to
ask why / do I want / to ask why / is there another / excuse / reason / or is it
just / I want to know / which of them were actually brave enough / to say it
to my face / here / now

A Letter to My Father

Judy Cuellar

Daddy,

Today I realized I've fully forgiven our past together. I see you fully as you are. I see the goodness in you. I see the wounded warrior, the wounded child. Does this mean that this forgiveness will magically transform the past into the fantasy of my dreams of what it would have been like to have my father fully healed, present, love and care for me as if I were the most priceless gift he had ever been given? No. Its taken me until 2 weeks before my 44th birthday to feel the fullness of release of our generational burden of internalized loathing of self, our people, our culture, our ancestors, our brilliant creative minds and our innate magic.

As a little girl, I was always so proud that you were my dad. In spite of my longing for you to show me and help me define my own value. You were the first man to break my heart. Such a gregarious spirit that yearned to soar so high above the clouds. An eagle who wasn't allowed to be what he was created to be. I see the scars of the many attempts to subdue and obliterate your wild, free, innate gift to fly and roam freely.

I see how you were the "whipping boy" simply for your inquisitive streak, the natural way it came to you to question the integrity of the system. And I see how they tried to beat any ounce of self-confidence you seemed to gain along the way. Not only in your own family which was only a microcosm within the unrelenting brutal regime of white supremacy and capitalism.

I understand why you drove yourself to harden until you became unrecognizable to yourself. You suffered great loss, guilt, shame under an oppressive and toxic system that was created to ensure your complete and utter failure and disillusionment. One that was only intended to deplete you and yet somehow you learned how to fortify yourself.

You are the eagle they trained to focus on the steel bars in front of you, north. Only allowing you to pace from east to west so that it would create a false sense of freedom and all the while there were no steel bars above or south of you. Each experience of pain and trauma reinforced you to continue to look north through the steel bars. Fervently, you tried to manipulate your body in every imaginable form in an effort to escape. The cold bars won every time. How could your flesh and blood manipulate itself in such a way to conquer the cold, harsh and immovable depths of a system, a place in which it is guaranteed that you will never have any advantage of gaining your footing.

Within this system your hands were forced to assimilate into the colonial mold or you die; slow or quick. Death is void of soaring and chasing dreams that fill the belly of your soul to overflowing.

South, the motherland. The motherland that birthed your irreverent fire. A fire, a strength that was built in spite of oppression. The motherland whose melancholy longing can be seen in your brown skin. We are made in their image. You were forced, they were forced to forget their origin, their greatness, their native tongue. And you were sure to pass this on to your children to ensure they wouldn't endure the same shame that had imprisoned you. In fact, it created broken children who would grow to end the generational trauma that had been passed down as a fraudulent family heirloom for centuries but that story is for another time.

In turn, you unknowingly passed on these insidious belief systems to your own children and resented them in their purest form of innocence. You had a hand in birthing eaglets that were constant reminders of the steel bars you resented yet found solace in. These eaglets were born without the sense that they could fly. You see, they grew to believe that they were only comprised of the steel bars that caged you. They were cages. Now they see their true from, their true magnificent glory as the eagles they were created to be.

For me, time and experience has taught me how to heal myself from these engrained belief systems and bold face lies. I know to a certain extent it has also been kind to you in that you are beginning to see the beauty and goodness in us. You may never be able to fully connect with us in this realm.

Sometimes, the damage is simply irreparable. However, I see you. I fully see you and how you came to be who you were and who you are. Do I have all the answers, or can I presume I truly know what it was like to be Juan Francisco Cuellar born on December 8th, 1954, to migrant workers and the middle child of ten? No. My gift has been empathy and the ability to see beyond what our eyes can affirm as real. I feel my way through this existence. I see you, Daddy, and I love you.

sweet tea (Southern Kitchen)

Kaia Valentine

i was eating catfish with my mom in Southern Kitchen, drinking sweet tea sweeter than sublime, when some young waitress, some long haired, beautiful waitress dropped a tray of ice water.

the old couple, the old, white-haired, white-skinned, couple, sat next to us. the man wore a proud Vietnam veterans t-shirt. if you know where this story is going, thank you for your service.

this man, this heavy-set, bearded, stereotypically masculine, man, jumped from his seat like he was keen to win the kangaroo Olympics. this man jumped like he just won the fear lottery. this man jumped like grenades and shrapnel flew through time into the vibrant, hallowed halls of Southern Kitchen.

God bless her, his wife, his instant remedy wife, his anchor bound by him by a near-senile, stunning, wedding ring, grabbed his plump arm and whispered silk love into his ear. he calmed at her touch, flushed blood-scarlet, and he apologized to us and to the shaken-up, humiliated waitress.

that's American boys: they'll go to war, kill anyone they have to, and when they get home, apologize for failing to be bullets shaped like men.

Genesis

Lev Pouliot

You came,
tarnished her brilliant gold,
coated her melanin shame
in your unfreckled   sun-fearing   flesh

You came into
spill and swell
holy water over psalm grotto rock-milk,
drank the salt sea   wave by wave

God flooded that legend   for good reason,
made all the saviors slaves.

You came into this
spoiled-cream ocean churning
with yellow life, got
the already globes of the yawning moon
sick   with   child

Came into this world, defiled
woe in the heaving tides,
morning too bright
unleavened white bread yeast taste
a sour back of your throat day
in the heat you Spoil.

In the other Genesis,
      Mary drinks herbs and kills you

My father yells at confederate statues

Katharine Threat

We are in Chattanooga, Tennessee. Lookout Mountain watches sleepily from the horizon, over land where generation after generation has loved, cured, buried each other. My genes are woven into the dirt. History from before legibility.

The summer is green and lush and beautiful, and curls damp with sweat stick to my ears and neck. Someone, somewhere, is always playing music, and someone, somewhere, is singing along. The air smells of barbecue and blooming trees. There are tour buses heading to the plantations near the river. We are not on them.

There is a white man, my father tells me, many generations ago, who snuck into the smooth brown bark of the family tree. I forget this information for years, being too young to understand the implications, to hold a mirror to generational trauma and face the patterns on the other side.

We are passing an old graveyard and the sky looks like rain. My father yells at confederate tombstones to remind them that they lost, and I am too young to yell with him. I am not yet angry enough. We return to black neighborhoods with black mothers and pick berries together, dark and sweet.

White Sons

Lauren Hoogkamer

White sons came out of my brown body
A body that loves them more than me
And I tell them you're still brown boys inside
Don't white-wash away the stories of our history
But I worry that they will learn to blend
Erase the memories of our diaspora
Forget to stand in solidarity with other brown boys
Forget to love brown girls like me
But they tell me they're a little bit white and a little bit brown
And I tell them we are the stories piled up inside us –
Omission can be worse than lies
My sons tell me I that am beautiful
And I try to forget all the white boys who said I wasn't

US
Kaia Valentine

A diner waitress wakes in the Midwest. America's the grease stain on her tired apron. Truckers smuggle intimacy, tuck their peckers into glory holes in the men's room, and pretend Dolly Parton's on the other side. Tires tread their years to pieces. Processed sugars seal their tragic fate. America, turn your radios on and listen to them. This ocean sized pool of corporations, ignorance, and super-PACs might be the same reason my mother's getting old before her days. My daddy doesn't feel like he deserves a dentist.

Men in overalls produce food that's thrown out. The cogs keep churning, and the shareholders get rich. American women in their battle armor: military camo, high heels, galoshes for docks, and salted fish secretions on their panties. If she works all day, why should she still smell nice?

The air's filled with palpable melancholy, 1950s nostalgia, milkshakes, tuna melts, and whatever perfume Melania wears. Some girl in South Carolina learns to play guitar. Her pick looks like a pistol to some good ol' boy. He fills her head with his mysterious sickness made of lead and copper. Her black body's in a mass grave. The grave marker says, "God bless the good: U.S."

Water

Ghazal for Dead Friends Who Still Have Facebook

Lev Pouliot

Djinn w/ those underwater welder eyes,
        Deep as Kentucky cave or Montana mine, saw

Ourselves as divine. Yearly pilgrimage
        Yearning for fleeting dragon chase. For juniper pine.

Burn first the motorcycle fuel.
        Your mother made me promise to keep you safe.

If these letters I burned never make it back to Dickinson County,
        They will find you on the road. Load up, roll thunder   Home.

Never got a better relationship w/ the water, just close enough to side-eye
        On careful rocks, a silhouette.

Hollowed out your gasp is palms-tight, a hard-earned waterfall
        still Can't swim, not even in   Your nightmares.

Hand, lung, grip
        Mine like steering wheel. Mine like

Steel trap. The world abandoned you. Heard you died by your own
        Hand

Me the map and I'll navigate, might
        Still drive up to Iron Mountain and look for you.

heavy.

Saiyare Refaei

heavy.

How be your heart?
My heart be heavy.
Heavy as this head
That can't seem to part
from the pillow.
Heavy as the lead
in these feet
finding footing with
each new day of uncertainty.
Heavy as the dread
of nostalgia eating away
in the pit of this stomach.
Heavy as the shred
of dreams still
anchoring this spine.
My heard be heavy.
And I am here
if you should need
anything.
Be well friends.
Know you are not alone
in this world, in this life.
Our time here
is too short
to prolong lonely.
No matter how you
Be
Feeling,
I am here.
If you should need
anything.
Even if that need be
nothing.
My heart be heavy.
How be your heart?

Please know it hurts

Paula Davidson

Please know it hurts
The extracting and sorting
Is it your pain or mine?
You push me to believe I'm fine
Please, take back your book of lies
Know it hurts to share some parts of humanity
Leave me in despair

I reach to find, myself, care
The systems taught me I shouldn't dare
This too short
That too long
I hear it thinks I'm doing it all wrong

I ask,
"Hey systems, you really think I was born to sing your song?
Have you considered where you went wrong?
What in the fuck taught you to expect me to follow along?"

Let's get real here
Hear this as my reveal
I know the songs it sings are shallow, skin deep,
Sung to gaslight and make me weak.

No, you typically don't hear me make a peep
Unless it's for my peeps
My love for y'all runs deep.

We are rivers to oceans of our freedom
Streams of tears
Waterfalls of love
Creeks of kindness
Full bodies
Flowing into bodies
Made to last
Built to rise
Turning the tides
Bringing to light the darkness that hides

Get ready
Stay steady
Without each other
We have next to nothing on the ride.

Untitled

Tina Văn

I am hard on myself
So hard that the pressure of the world
Cannot compare to what
      I endure

laps

gloria joy kazuko muhammad

been fighting with our fists up
generational trauma won't let up

flower baths, hot tea
ain't self care
for the dehumanized, you see

subliminal messages
yes, here, evergreen trees

still gotta carry batons
labor, perform

in a stomach that only weeps
self-care, how do we take care

those who caretake, can't take care

oppression, subconscious
an ocean, forever lost in

flower baths, hot tea
ain't self care
for the dehumanized, you see

will you speak, tongue to rhythm

does your fist even make a beat
for black & brown & in-between

you can name streets on fire
but can't name yourself

you can name streets on fire
but can't name trauma

flower baths, hot tea
ain't self care
for the dehumanized, you see

no grandfather's cabin
for us to retreat

no lounge chair
for daisies to engulf me

our knuckles been swollen
awareness, your privilege

trying to live
is our existence

as your hands submerge in bubble baths
and your knees shake from yoga poses

freedom will come from those
who put awareness to action

make living a sanction

we are defining the times
we are living in

Imprint

Brandi Douglas

If I am magic,
which I am.

If I am spirit,
which I am.

If I am love,

which I am.

How then, world, can you possibly erase me?

Me in the air,

Me in the soil,

Envisioned in my Ancestor's dreams,

Me, as history.

Spreading far and wide,

Like seeds, or ash.

So when I cross over and am held up against a looking glass,
You will still see what it means to be still and moving at the same
time.

Here and gone, a fluid entity.

Like water.

Like sustenance.

DNA, speaking only the language of revival.

H2O before you go

Paula Davidson

Don't drink from stagnant water.
I, being 70% water,
am building a connection to reveal that the same is made from man.
Do not absorb the weight of a stagnant person
for their nutrients have been depleted
and the lack of motion brews sickness.
Move with moving people.
Be like water, in action, its reaction is to flow.
Always.

Yi de Cuellar

Judy Cuellar

My roots run deep into the earth's core where an unrelenting fire burns

My spirit rises high above and beyond what our eyes can see

The soul of my existence can be seen in vibrant melodic colors that are interwoven with yours

Felt in ways that soothe the spirit as it envelopes you in the opulent warmth of self-indulgence

My sanctuary

Double Parked
Paula Davidson

You worked to get ahead, I hope, and with that opportunity it looks like you have chosen to remind others that they aren't where you are.

Well, you sir, are alone. Your nice car that you deem worthy of two spaces remains worn in one seat. Yours. You made it! To what, ride alone?

We here are up and coming.
Still working to get to a place where we can expand and put time into more of our loves.

We don't do this alone, though.
Those of us who have cars fill them with warm hearts so we can all get places, not in competition but on the rise.

We sprout in different places, realizing that our journeys are interconnected and relatable. That is not by accident.

My friend wakes up fighting his conscience trying to find a place for someone like you.

You're not good nor bad, in your own right, but the way you choose to move impacts those who feel and live around you.

Give us our space.

Mixed

Lauren Hoogkamer

Multicultural, biracial, mixed, mestiza
Ethnicity, ethnocentric, anomaly
Race, culture, identity
Your blood mixed with mine
The historiography of my parents' sexuality
The power play between two shades of brown
Descriptions, constructions, definitions—

I am not a conglomeration of labels
Races put on like cloaks
Stripped down into stereotypes
Condensed for people who are not me.
Not just two halves of what you can't see
You want to know me?
Then ask.

I am the only one with eyes that see this view
You don't know what my hands can do
Your heart has never loved who I loved
Your brain never thought the thoughts I think
Your feet don't plod the path I trod.

I am multidimensional, multi-intentional, multi-generational
So much more than multiracial
Yes, my blood is multinational
It may be rich but it's still red
So much more than a statistic
Of colored people who shared a bed.

Commotion

Brandi Douglas

Trust me, I've tried to walk briskly past grief
in hopes that it would not see me.

But we can't tiptoe around our trauma, can we?

Wrap avoidance like a blindfold around our heads and hearts,
it catches us, like it always does.

Shaking us awake in no subtle manner,

Begging to be seen.

So if you need to grieve, wrap it around you.

Walk heavy footed. Make a commotion.

Shout, "shame, in the wake up my
pain, has no home here!"

Because today,

today, it's okay to hurt.

To unravel to all four corners of the room,

and recognize that all the pieces of your broken heart will come together
again through the magnetism of your spirit.

But first, let's come undone.

Let's cry. Let's ache. Let's shout. Let's shake.

Let's grieve.
Let's grieve.
Let's grieve.

Untitled
chanel athena e.

some flowers
      sprout reaching
      for sun.
some flowers
      bloom
      with sweet
      syrup.
some flowers,
      squeezed
      in darkness
      &
      hung to dry,
      continue.

Sister's Stream of Consciousness

Kellie Richardson

1.

They separated me from my body. Body snatchers. Just like the movie...
jettisoned, apart from my essence. Devoid of my foremothers' intentions
and their due. Commodified in service to. Erased in reverence of. I fill the
holes with others. I harvest the best of others and try to make it my own.
Refined Frankenstein. I'm stitched together but I never really learned how
to sew.

I once suffered from Stockholm post-traumatic sister-friend syndrome.
Now it's more of a Munchausen's vibe – I have been caring for this sick girl
forever. How do I come to stop now?

2.

I always assume my lack.

It's become as much a part of me as my name. My name makes no sense.
A big booty black girl named Kellie? Actually, a middle-aged Black auntie
named Kellie. But Megan told me I could be a hot girl too though. I really
want to. It looks fun as fuck. Liberating. I want to be liberated. Can I do
that alone? Can I liberate my body from the narrative of others? It's written
all over me – rules scribbled in red as recipes, reminders, curses, warnings.
Memos in green for guidelines and acceptable conventions. A swath of
footnotes underlined in black to codify transgressions and sanctions.

How do I scrub them off? Can I? Who would I be without them? Would
I even recognize myself? Their stories about my body are both a map and a
noose.

I record my own notes and conclusions with invisible ink – on my heart so
the others can't see.

3.

This road is a series of settlings: Down into my bones, toward a solid center.
Forgiving and embracing the lesser versions. Adjusting requests. Less trials,
more errors. An erosion of indoctrinations:

Polished. Together. Poised. Worthy.

I strain my eyes to recognize what is still there, still possible, still fertile. I sometimes see it when the sunlight hits my sleepy eyes. First thing in the morning. From the bathroom mirror. I catch my reflection. I'm struck by myself. I'm smitten and seduced. By my beauty and fortitude. Feeling for myself what I adore in the great ones.

But it rains a lot here. The sun is busy elsewhere and I'm left to my own devices.

The manual says I meet some of the criteria– a scar at the base of my belly, skin that distended to leave a trail that proves someone once wanted me. My spine a string of pearls and trick wire. I bleed so beautifully it's become my honor. I'm a fence and a field. Preaching the scripture and breaking commandments.

Like the Crane Wife

Lydia K. Valentine

To keep becoming a woman is so much self-erasing work.
– CJ Hauser, *The Paris Review*

My feathers are a thick blanket of needful truth.
They sigh, achingly smooth against my faithless fingers
as I pluck them out. Every night,
each one sways a slow, silent goodbye
down to the surface of the water,
seeking a final touch but finding only my rippled
reflection, this stranger, this untruth I am becoming
with each extracted feather.

I don't look.

There is, somewhere, a tangled mass of me,
all of the self I've sacrificed to be safe,
to take up less of the space deemed
for those of other shapes, other skins,
to keep becoming a woman,
a human being,
in their eyes.

Truths

Jami Williams

Hands pressed on the fridge
Forehead pressed on a window in my shower
Vibrator pressed on 8,000 orgasms

Kids scream outside at midnight
For the boom that shakes windows
Before dawn

Makes a car alarm scream
Hiding in the dining room
While the baby sleeps in his crib

Gnawing on toes to soothe the ache
Hauling breath in a sling
To fight the labor it takes

To be a mother
With a womb so empty
From the beating of a drum

The magician filled me
With normal abilities
Tubes shedding screams to

Feel me
Holding long enough
So the dough doesn't deflate

Wondering what it feels
Like to break a cloud meant
For sopping up rage

Punctured nipples dried out
Warmth in the most
Random places

Bruised by every hail stone
No coincidences exist
Where we meet

The Sound of a Heartbeat

Marisha McDowell

Born in a quiet, foreign place
Alone and abandoned
No cigars, no beers or newborn lace

A life begun with no one
Dejected and sober
No luck found here,
Not even a four-leaf clover

Deserted down a backstreet
The only sound is a lone heartbeat
And still my core is filled with fear
Hoping against hope that someone would celebratory cheer

The darkness never seems to end
Hark, I hear
The sound of a drum starts to transcend
A life worth living has just been born
I realize I am no longer forlorn

I start to feel an anthem and I must abide
This parade continues to march solidified
This performance is no rehearsal
Not a chance is had of reversal
A thump, thump, thump guides each day
My future is not defined by this alleyway

Angel from Hell

Marisha McDowell

Remember that time I stayed quiet
Though in my heart of hearts all I wanted to do was riot
My world had begun to be tipsy
Round and round from too much whiskey

You called yourself my guardian angel
Filling my head with lies and deceit
It was much too late that I had realized
Oh boy am I in danger
You had no intent to be sweet

I never wanted to play that game
Little did I know
This was your claim to fame
We started to undress
The memories are faded and not all there
Though what happened next indeed, isn't hard to guess

My brain didn't know what to do
Escape occupied my mind
I didn't want to cum, too
Kung fu
Out of this space
Into a marathon pace
Kick you, slap you
All until you're blue in the face

Finally, I was feeling less groggy
Realizing what had happened to my body
Your time has come
Goodbye I started to shout
Don't ever take advantage of a girl's blackout

bone soaked tired

Kaia Valentine

Buckle in. You're drowning. Look. A small pocket of dwindling air. Swim to it. Wedge your head above a brutal, homicidal death. Breathe, babygirl, and reminiscence on times you took your breath for granted. Oxygen's running out. You're going to have to move.

You have to move. Your alarm's chirping morning birdsongs. If you don't get up, you're going to be late. You paint a mental picture of your morning routine. Check phone. News says Eric Garner, George Floyd, Freddie Grey, Breonna Turner. Brush teeth, dress yourself, attempt to gobble down a decent living. But you haven't moved, and you're exhausted. Heaven and Hell rest on both weight-bearing shoulders. You choose to roll over, drift back into a deep, depressed sleep. Workday be damned. What can you do? You're drowning. Bone Soaked. Buckle in.

Emergency Room Rant

Katherine Felts

What my white family doesn't seem to understand:
Is that no matter how many times I demand
to be heard, there is always some nurse
who knows my body better than I do.
A doctor who's much smarter than I.
And should I cry out in pain – the sound
is met most often with surprise, that
one such as I might feel the same things.
Though I rarely have anything to gain ...
My symptoms are often blamed on attention
seeking and overthinking my situation, so
I resist the temptation to scream *very* often.
It sometimes feels like cotton in my throat.
A blockage, stoppage, a vote against
my own self. It doesn't help that
these people just don't give a shit.
To sit here and suggest I'm an
intravenous drug user,
as if that's the worst kind of abuser
I could be. I mean –
YES! I'd like to feel good, too.
That's why I came to you.
Instead, I'm
writing another angry poem,
Wishing I was home, not
wasting in a pale blue gown, again –
How do I know their medicine is working?
I believe that I don't deserve help.
Take every chance to put my needs on a shelf,
to forget about me.
This broken body travels well –
old reliable, it's got stories left to tell.
I think.
God, I hope there's mileage
left at the end of the rage.
I'm trying every day to ensure

my survival. Knowing that
thrive or *cure* is not planned for me.
I guess this has just been a rant.
I'll recant the harsh words I said.
I'm sorry!
Of course, I love our healthcare workers!
They're here to keep... some of us safe.
And I'm willing to die
for their right
to deny me my place on the earth.
For what it's worth, I'm not stopping, though.
No, you can still catch me
trying not to abandon things I love,
trying to keep up, to meet what
I imagine the expectations for me are.
Don't read this as a concession.
It's just a confession that I'm tired.
But I guess that's the (c)harm of being a Black woman.

Untitled

Tina Văn

Yes, that is who I used to be
It is not the person you see
You see a shadow of my being
   Behind me
But, I am facing the light
    We do not see in the
      Same dimension

Don't let them cloud your perception

Jasmine Hernandez

You can see clearly now
How every piece fits
What was given versus
What you already had
Who was their Jesus to you?
When you called the Sun – Savior
When you called God – Creator
Ask yourself,
Does your body need a Doctor
Or Mother?
Manmade or nature?
Don't look too far in the wrong direction
You already know the answer

What I come with
Is from those who came before me
What I come with
Is not for your consumption
What I come with
Is everything I need for where I'm going

homeward bound

Eileen Jimenez

I feel embodied in water
expanded in water
alive in water
filled by water
held by water
powerful in water
protected by water
weightless in water
seen by water
myself in water

loved by water
my first home.

Untitled

chanel athena e.

nostalgia
      sleeps peacefully without
            night terrors or monsters.
    instead, dreams are compartmentalized
      organized and stores to be well
            preserved.

    spoonful, after spoonful,
       memories refined, enjoyed are repeated
    no notice of renovation.

until the presence of thought is
               absent.

      abruptly
         interrupting.

Sky

Green

Cervantes Gutierrez

Green as the journal full of unpolished poems
Green as the smell of Sugar Cane in a hot May afternoon
Green as the hierba buena my Abuelita uses to make remedios
when my stomach hurts
Green as the dying plants in my neighbors' balcony
Green, I want to be loved in green
Green as the white men paper with white men pictures
The ink of my pen is green filing another government document to let me
stay. Needing green to get through another interview where I have to
repeat I'm no alien, but all they see is green.
How is this green different from the other green?
If my people existed in high mountains and now we are here by the sea.
Because the waters of the rivers inside me are green
A prayer is green
and in the land of rebirth, I become
green.

Lover

Kim Archer/Leah Tussing

When I saw you today
I knew there was more I needed to say
But the words wouldn't leave my lips
I was paralyzed with it

I silently screamed
you should never have doubted
You closed off your heart to me
while I quietly shouted

Lover, this is my letter to you
These are the last words
That my heart has gone through
I can keep movin on
Cuz that's what you do
But the back of my mind has a place just for you

I tried to be
What you needed from me
Now that's done
And we're both moving on
I can't help but wonder
Feel like it's pulling me under
We're both moving on, my lover
To where and where from

Lover, this is my letter to you
These are the last words
That my heart has gone through
I can keep movin on
Cuz that's what you do
But the back of my mind has a place just for you

Did you think you could run
Think you'd easily part
With no wounds and no scars
In these games of the heart

Lover, this is my letter to you
These are the last words
That my heart has gone through
I can keep movin on
Cuz that's what you do
But the back of my mind has a place just for you
Lover...

About the Heart

Jasmine Hernandez

The way we love people
Crazy, relentless
Sometimes tragically
Is how I want to fall in love with my art
Is how I want you to wake up
Excited, ready for life
Is how I want to take to heart
Every miracle around me
And love to live life
The way we love people

American Dreams

Lev Pouliot

My first anti-racist lesson was that people are generally not to blame for their miseries. Blackness, as a kid, meant the smell of Pink Lotion—which I could really use to calm my frizzing hair even now, as Washington see-saws between the humid season and the season where ash becomes new weather from mountainous fires that I fear will consume someone who has never allowed himself to be consumed by anything. I remember seeing a friend's mom pull her shirt up in the kitchen, tiger-claws etched in her deflated skin from childbirth, and the dark line, narrow but perceptible, that bifurcated her multiracial body.

"What is that?" I whispered in reverence, too surprised to be shy. Her unselfconsciousness with her body had me awe-stricken. Maybe it meant I could be bold too. "Honey, it's just my line. All of us dark girls got one. You got one too, see?" And her pink acrylics lifted my shirt before I could protest, pointing out the faint boundary that separated me neatly down the center into two.

How had I never noticed before? This was the first time I remember arguing for my Blackness. I'd gone up to my mom later, excited about my new identity, proudly showing her my line and what it meant and asking if she had one too. Her reaction was chilly. It was a distance she achieved from a combination of her schizophrenia and trauma—repeating the same wounds over and over,
re-stretching them like dough—and her fear of corruption, of others, of someone being co-opted by another and turned against her. Eyes slightly off-gaze, lips thin and set; she swallowed my excitement like a poison. I wasn't allowed to go back there for a while.

When I did, Miss Jordan was covertly pissed in her way, holding a grudge eternally against my mother that was revealed in her snide comments, though she was too proud to be taking it out seriously on a ten-year-old. Any perceived slight sent my mom into a letter-writing maelstrom, the ultimate leverage of white-woman bitchiness. She got haughty and secretarial, yet her standoffish "To Whom It May Concern's" betrayed by her tendency to delve into psychotic non-sequiturs. I knew Miss Jordan had gotten one of these, and I was embarrassed and grateful to be in her presence in the aftermath.

My mom would brag about the whitest shit—that I was "a genius," that I cleaned friend's houses when I went over—and pull me away by the arm whenever I showed interest in hip-hop music oozing from low-key Cadillacs, insisted borrowing was a mortal sin, and called our weed-smoking neighbors (in none-too-quiet words) drug addicts. "Don't dance to their music," she would tell me.

Identity – identity is a funny fucking thing. Humans like to pretend they formed themselves out of the dirt sometimes, but we're all our attractions and resistances to others. Desire is the basest element of physics, and it can't exist without tension—which in turn can't exist without dimension. A fatherless punk, I am no more Black than I am French-Canadian than I am Mexican (because I am so often coded that way). My self is what was formed from pulling away from the people I didn't want to be; it is enveloped in the context of how I am seen. Maybe this is why "non-binary" appeals to me as a gender identity: it encompasses my reactionary nature and the obvious shortcomings of a mutual either/or decision.

When you hold an identity that is rooted in your refusal to play by the rules, it brings you crashing into consciousness of what the rules actually are. Like most teenagers, I was too cool for authority. Authority responded by trying to push me out of my youth and into a firm identity as soon as possible, rolling its eyes right back at me.

"Get a job" was the refrain that accompanied that mannerism, in the way of their parents before them, exhausted with the entitled disconnection from the world of struggle and capitalist demands under which they were besieged. And sometimes, the kids got the job, shelving library books or scooping ice cream a la The American Dream.

I didn't. Not until I was eighteen and had already graduated. I was home-schooled, and often my mom and I would get a lot of weird looks or pointed questions in public when I was younger, like *shouldn't they be in school?* My mom wasn't an eye-roller, but she got exhausted by fielding all those questions. And although they weren't asked to me directly, as a teenager I could feel those same folks wondering: *isn't it time for them to get a job?* If Blackness is scrutinized, sometimes I feel like mixed-ness is even more so, because it lacks the clarity of easy categorization. If I was Black, they would know my place in the social order. As a mixed kid I was always being pressured to show up more for one group or the other through my clothes, attitude, idiolect, hobbies, accent, hair, body. I always found it easier to downplay my Black characteristics and emphasize the white ones: I straightened my hair, performed well in school, and after high school—complete with the eye roll—got a job. I performed whiteness. And for the most part, I was pretty happy with it, as people with a certain amount of power afforded to them tend to be.

But like most teenagers, I also didn't have a lot of agency, and although I would have fought this idea (as we all do): some of my decisions were not my own. And what kept me from one specific decision wasn't lack of effort, initiative, or employability: it was a restriction placed on the government assistance my mother received.

Our housing was paid for through a federally administered voucher. It's called Section 8, and operates as a sliding-scale housing subsidy which, for us, covered the entirety of our rent for the 2-bedroom apartment we lived in. She made under $8k a year from her disability checks from SSI, which paid for her car payment and insurance, utilities, and necessities. It was common for me to find her at the dining room table at strange hours, scrawling figures in notebooks to estimate her income down to the penny. We kept the water heater turned off except for special occasions, and carefully moderated the electric bill to less than $20 a month. When I talked to her about getting a job, she was horrified, because it meant that her already-scant income would be reduced, and I'd have to pay her to make up the difference.

In case you don't know, the federal poverty line in 2006—when I was a freshman in high school—was $13,200. If you'd told me that I was poor, I would've believed you, but rolled my eyes. Our food stamps were supplanted with regular trips to the food bank and—prior to my tween years—waiting in line at the soup kitchen. After fifteen, I was too embarrassed to be seen at the Salvation Army, which was right across from my alma mater, Battle Creek Central High School, until it was later demolished and rebuilt in hopes of pulling students from wealthier neighborhoods. Sure, we were poor, but we weren't *destitute.* My mom was *crazy,* but not like the man she visited who hoarded old magazines and muttered constantly about his trauma. We washed our clothes in the bathtub and hung them on racks—clothes that were supplanted with a yearly voucher to the Charitable Union, where you could mindlessly sift through sorted bins of yellowing used undies, peculiar Halloween costumes, and dogeared paperbacks. At least that's what we did until I learned to shoplift. I was already a sinner with my consumerist instincts. But there was always someone doing worse than us.

Like the car. An obvious status symbol. When I was little, we were lucky enough to live four blocks away from a grocery store, which is still a trek for a single disabled mother and a small child in a Michigan winter. We got the car when I was six. It meant no more bus rides that smelled like human shit and desperation—no old men with fat weather-cracked hands smiling their fake smiles. We could exist in our own isolated bubble, complete with heat.

We all know the narrative: "In America, if you work hard, you will succeed. So those who do not succeed have not worked hard."

Ralph Waldo Emerson, a classic American author well-known and loved for his work on Transcendentalism, was a pivotal figure in advancing this idea, and its relationship to class. Merging Transcendental ideals with German romanticism, and weaving in copious themes of proto-English racial chauvinism, he published works that spoke to a supposed *inherent nature* that defined Anglo-Saxons in the modern world: in addition to beauty, virility, and longevity, he attributed them *freedom* as a racial characteristic. Naturally free. This description, which attested that "the instinct for liberty" was an inherent Saxon trait, completely ignored the slavery that was present on American soil and in British colonies, and also the very recent history of indentured servitude. The irony, it seems, was lost on him.

By making freedom a racial trait, this meant the burden of freedom laid with the enslaved, impoverished, or marginalized peoples—not with those who oppressed them. "These sorts of assumptions about the poor are an American phenomenon." Emerson's obsession with fate ignored the sociopolitical realities of the 1850s; to him, an inalienable character trait was what kept Blacks as an enslaved class, loomed over poverty-stricken Irish immigrant families, and made Native Americans unworthy of the power held by social advancement.

Max Weber laid out the impact of this fairly well when he said "no one in favored circumstances wants to admit the chanciness of privilege." An early twentieth-century sociologist, Weber spoke to the factors behind racial-ized hierarchy: a combination of our psychological desires for free will and personal agency mixed with a social impetus to define the "natural" and underived quality that made them deserve the power and wealth they found themselves with.

We had just begun moving away from skull-measuring, but the practice of co-opting science to validate our subjective worldview hadn't left the textbooks, nor the minds of those with the greatest intellectual authority. Psychology is at play here too. Humans, especially when they are feeling defensive, are more prone to see the shortcomings of others as indicators of their attitude or being, rather as products of their circumstance.

What does it mean to be a racist? It's a tenuous accusation, in a world where a good deal of racism manifests itself as participation in racist systems, or benefiting from an enforced racial order. "Our family never owned slaves," my mother always told me, proudly. "We aren't racist."

Yet within this deep insistence, there was an unexamined fear. She led me away from cars blasting hip-hop with a stern admonition "not to dance to *their music*." Media consumption was already tightly patrolled within our house, but I knew without asking that bringing her a movie with Black people on the cover would trigger her sensibilities. She hated everything Black in color or associated with Blackness.

"The color of the devil," she said, with thin lips, from behind her Jehovah's Witnesses pamphlets. Apocryphal resurrectionists whose whiteness manifested in casseroles and excommunication, they had the most boring service of all the churches I'd been in, right down to their bland psalms, nondescript prefab buildings, and total abhorrence for all holidays. I was seven.

I liked mustard sandwiches, Power Rangers, and rabbits. I had just had my first sex dream, which involved nothing more innocuous than the rush of see-sawing with my only friend, a mixed boy named Tory—but I woke up with my ass and thighs steaming hot like I'd just emerged from the bath. I was already a sinner. Anyone who's ever hung out with a kid can probably attest to their intense desire for fairness, and I was no different.

She told me sex was bad, yet I knew she had it; I also knew she didn't like it. She also told me that lying was bad, but either she was lying about enjoying sex, having it, or both. She'd exposed me to the idea of "white lies," which of course is just adult shorthand for a way to break your own rules without facing the consequences or more deeply examining your moral propensities. So I wasn't too impressed with her moralizing at me, but it didn't always strike me as incongruous that she had a special affection for Black men.

For the longest time, her apparent distaste for sex had led me to believe that I was a child of rape. White mom, mixed kid, Black rapist. The narrative is gross, but not unfamiliar. And the actions of the Black men she dated all confirmed it a little, so while I distrusted her interpretation of the world to a massive degree, I still remembered the parts that confirmed it. Michael over the-knee spanking me the first time I met him, his first time in *my* house: age five. Steve narc'ing on me when I was reading at the dinner table, leading my mom to rip up my favorite book: age ten. She was afraid of them, and that made me afraid, but it took me years to find out that her fear was shame about being something she didn't want to be.

"Liberals," offers Matthew Desmond in the New York Times article that spawned this memoir, "find themselves arguing about radical solutions... like a jobs guarantee...or a universal basic income."

Despite not identifying with Liberalism, I do want both of those radical solutions. But in doing so, I also need to acknowledge the reality of the past —and to be a better sociologist and historian than the white men who have defined what those fields mean. I need to validate the reality of my mother, who raised me—single-handed-ly through schizophrenia, multiple physical disabilities, and a brain injury—to be *exactly* the kind of person who questions the realities that are offered.

I need to question political leaders who "refuse to view child care as work" and who would champion solutions that demonize the most vulnerable members of society—who ought to be intelligent enough to see that it isn't just an *accident* that wealth distribution is violently unequal and inequitable, and ought to be both smart and kind enough to realize that neither individual mettle nor God-given raced-based traits are what prevent the most marginalized groups from seeking their freedom.

Individualism, in the sense that one person could manifest their own con-sequences, regardless of the circumstances around them, is a "white lie" per-petuated by those in power meant to keep those with less privilege spinning their own wheels in the cold January snow. It is a move played by those who refuse to play by their own rules. Don't believe me? Ask a teenager.

paving my path as a woman in physics

Kathleen Julca

Broken peltiers, my old fishbowl with a square-hole in the bottom, and a chunk of Americium-241 from my fire alarm (sorry mom) littered my table at one point. I have several battle wounds from a CPU fan on my hand, too.

I couldn't see too far into the future past the clutter of my desk. But I do know what brought me here: never quite being able to separate myself from physics, from gravity or electromagnetic energy bouncing around my room.

My teachers would ask, "And what do you wanna be when you grow up?"

"I'm going to be a theoretical physicist working on the ATLAS experiment in Geneva, Switzerland."

My school had zero physics classes and not even a science lab, but it didn't matter to me. Sheer effort could make up for anything. My friend even gave me his physics book, "Because the old thing was just gathering dust." But (insert high-school freshman squeal) I felt so lucky! I could finally do real physics!

Slowly but surely, the adventure and mystique of being a theoretical physicist came into reach. And out of reach again when the formulas and endlessly trailing numbers were too much. I would knead my frustrations into cookie dough and bring mindfulness back by playing Disney hits on Harry (The Flute).

But there was a sentiment that overcame my adrenaline from reading 'An Elegant Universe' and playing Disney songs. Shame, and it grew like weeds. Shame that Physicist Richard Feynman wouldn't want to work with me. Shame when my male counterparts boasted about the textbooks they finished and AP Physics C problems they could solve. Shame that I wouldn't be prepared for collegiate or novel work. I gave self-studying my energy even when already stretched thin, yet it didn't seem to be enough.

Just as my sky was falling, I turned to my textbook. My textbook. Those words soothed me as I landed on particle ionization - complex, intimidating, probably best for future-physicist-me. But I had seen it on YouTube... cloud chambers. I looked at models showcasing unique concepts, and maybe it was too many Hot Cheetos or a final attempt to regain my niche, but I started designing my chamber, and it felt surreal.

I joined communities of electrical engineering who helped me make meaning of peltiers, zip-ties, and coolant paste; the cloud chamber to me was like a supercomputer to professional gamers: a dream come true. Once conditions were just right, I poured in isopropanol-alcohol and there were magnificent wisps of energy. My hands, my design, made that? I was speechless.

I am proud to say I am pursuing novel work: building and experimenting on a plasma ray. I am most thrilled, though, to soon use it as a teaching tool for elementary schoolers, I would lug it anywhere and do anything to empower them towards their ah-ha moment. Physics makes me wonderfully frustratedly-excitedly dream big – paired with my knack for CS – I'll keep analyzing and formulating ideas that push the boundaries of my mind further every day.

Latina, Resurrected
Jesi Hanley Vega

It was August 19, 2017, and I was protesting racism. One week earlier, at a "Unite the Right" rally in Charlottesville, Virginia, a white nationalist drove his Dodge Challenger into the crowd and killed a counter protester named Heather Heyer. At the time, I was a leader in a local political action group and, hours after the attack, two young activists reached out to ask for my help in organizing a local protest. For the next few days they worked around the clock and, on the following Saturday, we gathered with a few hundred other protesters at Kandle Park on Tacoma's North side. Though the organizers had hoped to hold the event at People's Park in Tacoma's historically Black Hilltop neighborhood, our last minute mobilization meant that the only site available was on Tacoma's predominantly white North Side — a change in venue that meant a change in audience as well.

It was one of those summer days when it can seem like the whole city is out celebrating, so the energy was high even though the mood was somber. Addressing the crowd of mostly white protesters, local politicians and community leaders spoke out against racism, violence, and all the other sewage that had risen to the surface since the 2016 election. That sewage, which had been steaming beneath the surface of American society for generations, was a big surprise to a lot of white people, but no surprise at all to Black folks and other People of Color who'd been living with it all their lives. And it was no surprise to me. Though I'd been living in University Place, a fairly affluent area of West Tacoma, for almost five years, I'd grown up in The Bronx.

When the last speaker of the day, Mayor Marilyn Strickland[1], a Black woman, took the mic, I expected the usual: a fairly rousing, if politically safe, speech about overcoming differences and the power of the people. But, instead of sticking to the script, Mayor Strickland veered hard into "keeping it real" and asked that the People of Color come stand with her to face the audience. She wanted the whites in the crowd to take a good long look, to connect with the humanity of the people in front of them, and to remember that these were the people whose lives they were there to honor and protect. These were Tacoma's People of Color.

Standing on the grass near the mayor, I froze. As two crowds formed in front of me, I stayed right where I was as an uneasiness I'd been accustomed to tuning out, one I'd been suppressing for years, became impossible to

---

1 In 2020, Strickland was elected as US Representative (D) for Washington's 10th Congressional District.

ignore. In Mayor Strickland's moment of reckoning, I finally admitted to myself that I didn't know where I belonged.

***

My mother was born in Puerto Rico and moved to New York City when she was five.

Like me, my father, a mix of Jewish, German and Irish ancestry, had been born and raised in the Bronx. When I was a kid in the 70's, The Bronx was notorious for burning down, and when I was a teenager, it was known for crack,[2] but my neighborhood provided a relative sanctuary among otherwise dangerous streets. Known as "The Amalgamated," it was a Socialist housing cooperative that had been founded by Jewish trade unionists in the 1920's. By the early seventies, when its original founders had gotten old and their kids had moved away, the neighborhood was seeking fresh, new "cooperators." My parents, who'd first met on the subway,weren't the only young people to emerge from the sixties married to someone from another race or ethnicity so, together with a group of my dad's high school and City College friends, they joined the cooperative, eager to create a kind of radical, politically woke utopia for their young, mixed, families.

My memories of those years are alternately vivid and hazy: playing "Star Wars" with Douglas Hill (Black & Jewish), "Run, Catch, Kiss" with Peter Pinero (Black & Puerto Rican), and "Wilderness Family" in the park with the Stanton girls (Irish & Italian[3]). As in so many communities, our families picnicked, barbecued and discoed together, and I paid close attention as the dads argued loudly about sports and politics and the moms volunteered at the local food co-op. And then, at the onset of a new decade, I witnessed my entire neighborhood mourn the election of Ronald Reagan. Disgusted by the barely disguised racism of his campaign, my parents, their friends, and all our neighbors knew that his dual promises of trickle down economics[4] and a "war on drugs[5]" would cause even further disaster in poor areas like ours — and they did.

But while our block survived the Reagan administration, us kids couldn't stay in The Amalgamated forever. Regardless of race or ethnicity, our parents wanted better futures for the younger generation, and that

---

2 Of course, The Bronx is also known as the place where Deejay Kool Herc gave birth to Hip Hop at a house party on Sedgwick Avenue, just three miles down the road from where I grew up.

3 Even though Irish and Italians are considered equally "white" in mainstream American culture, there were still very real differences between the groups and the Stantons' was considered a "mixed"

4 a.k.a. reduction of social services

5 a.k.a. accelerated mass incarceration

meant educations that would take most of us out of The Bronx and into worlds that looked nothing like our neighborhood. In my case, those worlds consisted of Vassar College and The University of Chicago: elite, overwhelmingly white institutions where young people are rigorously groomed to take their places as the intellectual, artistic, political, and financial leaders of tomorrow – and uphold the inequality that dominates American culture.

***

So there I was in Kandle Park and Mayor Strickland seemed to be asking me personally, "Who are you? Are you that little girl growing up in The Bronx, eating gandules at abuela's house? Are you an Amalgamated kid, running around Van Cortlandt Park with your radical Black, brown, and Jewish friends? Or are you that stylish Vassar girl? That West side mom with the blue-eyed husband and the yoga practice? Are you brown? White? A Puerto Rican? A Jew? Or are you nothing?"

Despite my progressive upbringing, I'd grown up absorbing the cultural cues about race and ethnicity that American culture fed me – especially the ones about Latinas. I knew that Puerto Rican girls were hyper-sexualized bad-asses (and bad students[6]) so I did what I could to assure that white people liked and accepted me as their relatively modest, even-tempered equal. As a teenager, I'd made sure not to wear nameplate necklaces or bamboo hoops and, into my mid-twenties, worked to eliminate any trace of a distinctive Bronx accent. By the time I was an adult, I was fully accepted as white and most people had no idea who I "really" was or where I was from – unless the topics of race, class, or poverty came up. Then, in a self-righteous rage, I'd give myself away as a hot-blooded Latina and feel the ground I'd gained, as well as the misplaced trust I'd earned, slip away.

But radical politics aside, I did nothing to maintain a connection with other People of Color. Instead, in pursuit of the elusive "better life," I continued gravitating towards white environments which provided me with the resources and proximity to power I wanted — while rejecting whatever reminded me too much of the powerlessness I'd felt at home. In other words, just as my parents and all the other parents in our community had wanted, I was "living the American Dream."

But I was all fucked up.

---

6 When asked what she'd gotten on her SATs, Jennifer Lopez famously replied "nail polish." Love ya, Jenny from the Block!

Yes, I'd gotten myself out of The Bronx, gotten that excellent education, and traveled all over the world; yes, I'd had the privilege of following my passions as an artist and spiritual seeker. But I'd failed to achieve the fulfillment I'd been seeking and there was a fundamental way in which I still felt mute and powerless. Indistinct feelings of shame and guilt haunted me and, rather than take full advantage of the so-called "opportunities" around me, I suffered from recurring cycles of depression, anxiety, and confusion that left me feeling like I always had to start over; having mastered the habit of self-sabotage, I often did.

So, like I said, there I was, standing next to the mayor of Tacoma, 47 years old, and, once the initial panic had passed, considering that my dysfunction was related to this "divide into groups" thing, and that my chronic uneasiness – about race, being mixed, and seeming white – had messed with my mind more than I'd thought.

Moments later, it was my turn to take the mic. In a split second, I decided that, for the first time ever, I was going to speak this truth; I declared to the crowd that, not only was I the daughter of a Puerto Rican mother and a Jewish father, but that I was confused about it. I admitted that Mayor Strickland's request had touched a wound I didn't know I had and I told everyone there that day, everyone who had come out to protest Charlottesville, and Proud Boys, and Trump, and racism, that I didn't know where I belonged. Then I thanked Mayor Strickland[7] for giving me something to think about and, having made my public confession (which probably took less than a minute), I did what I was there to do; I thanked the speakers, acknowledged the organizers, and reminded everyone to call their Congresspeople.

***

Until that day in Kandle Park, people would often say to me, "What are you?" or "You're Puerto Rican? I never would have guessed," or "You're the whitest Latina I've ever met." And while they were busy thinking how cool or exotic that was, I would stammer, turn red, or look away. But after that day, I began taking steps to articulate my unique perspective as a Latina of mixed heritage. I began to understand why it mattered that I do that, and also discovered how much I wanted to support other marginalized people to do the same.

A few months after my moment at the mic, I began attending The Conversation[8], a weekly gathering in which Tacomans share personal

7 Upon writing this essay, I quietly freaked out when I learned that Mayor Strickland is also mixed. She is the daughter of an African American father and a Korean mother.
8 The Conversation is an outreach program of The University of Puget Sound's Institute for Race and Pedagogy and has met every Sunday in Tacoma for more than a decade.

experiences of race and educate themselves about the history and practice of racism in America. In that sacred space, I admitted how badly I'd always longed to talk about my experiences and was surprised by how much grief lay buried beneath my modest and even-tempered persona. I'd never before shared publicly about my childhood and I was startled by the intense vulnerability and fury I felt, not only about my heritage, but about growing up in a place where white landlords openly profited from burning down Black and brown neighborhoods. In telling these truths, and in witnessing other people's reactions to them, I discovered that these experiences, as well as my journey from one of the poorest areas in the US to some of the wealthiest, had given me a valuable perspective on race, economics, and caste[9]. That time I spent engaged with The Conversation taught me that the confusing circumstances of my youth, which had always felt like a curse, were a great gift, and I began speaking and writing about them more openly.

***

Within minutes of my speech, volunteers began dismantling the podium and taking down banners, and I started weaving a path through the crowd. I felt shaky about what I had just said, and I could feel my heart beating. Lost in a swirl of self-consciousness, I would have just walked straight to my car if it hadn't been for the protesters who began approaching me, one at a time. The first was the activist I'd been working with all week. She told me that she was mixed too (in delayed recognition I thought "oh! right!") and confessed to also feeling conflicted. Another protester told me that she'd written a book about her mixed Asian upbringing and now felt more at peace. And yet another gave me a hug. It wasn't at all what I'd been expecting. It wasn't even what I'd hoped for. But it was exactly what I needed.

In the years between graduating college and moving to Tacoma, I'd been presented with numerous opportunities that had seemed desirable on the surface: a fellowship here, an interested producer there, a fantastic job offer at a major studio over there. But to the dismay of my parents and the people who cared about me, I blew them up, one after the other, often only partially understanding what I'd done. Now I understood that these invitations to ascend in white society, as a white-ish person, on purely white terms, were not something my soul could accept.

There was a time when I thought the ambivalence and shame I felt about my racial and ethnic identity were insignificant, private matters which

9 Interviewed by NPR about her book "Caste," in August, 2020, author Isabel Wilkerson described the term "caste" as "more precise [than race]; it gets at the underlying infrastructure that often we cannot see, but that is there undergirding much of the inequality and injustices and disparities that we live with in this country."

would never be resolved and most certainly never revealed. It never occurred to me that, one day, I would change my own life, and my own definition of who I was, by speaking them out loud – not from a place of blame or victimhood, but from a place of curiosity and courage. By declaring, on that summer day in Tacoma, what I genuinely felt about who I genuinely was, I asserted my Latina identity as a political and spiritual act, and began to embrace new possibilities that were far different from the ones that had tormented me earlier.

These new possibilities have resulted in a different kind of life than the one I used to think I wanted. I'm still creative, but now my fulfillment comes not only from my own expression, but from nurturing and celebrating artists of color dedicated to expressing their truths, paradoxes and all. As an editor, a writing instructor, and a communications professional, I work joyfully to amplify voices of color because I know, firsthand, the difference it makes. This kind of truth telling brings liberation, it brings freedom and it brings change – not only to the story's tellers and listeners, but to the world.

What's Your Ethnicity?

Stasha Moreno

As usual for me, I'm at the grocery store on my lunch break, grabbing a sandwich to go. I brush my long dark hair out of my face as I grab a green tea from the cooler. I get in line to check out. My hazel eyes meet the cashier's brown eyes as he asks me, "Paper or plastic?" "No bag, please," I say as I enter my credit card into the machine. The cashier stares at me still, as he rings out my items. Holding my gaze for slightly longer than necessary. I smile and look down at the card machine. "What ethnicity are you?" The cashier asks me. This question catches me completely off guard. I was so angry at that moment. His question rolling off his tongue like it was just a comment on the weather, with a big smile on his face, and a twinkle in his eye.

Empathy for other folks who have been put in this situation came flooding to me. All of the awkward moments strangers have put "others" in. The people who don't look like them. The Brown people, the Black people, the people with accents, the people who for some reason maybe strike a little fear in someone, just enough fear to spark the question. You know the question I mean, "Just wondering, where are you from?" Now I'm sure you are thinking, "I'm not scared! I'm asking this because I'm generally interested in this person! I want to get to know them better, and so I'm asking where they are from. What, now I can't even ask a simple question?"

I think asking people where they are from is fine. In fact it can actually be helpful and lead to other conversations that can help you to get to know the person. However, if someone who looks different from you answers the question, "Where are you from?" with, "Seattle." Then you look confused, and say, "No, I mean where are you FROM?" You are putting that person on the spot and asking them questions about their race, ancestors, heritage and culture which you probably could not even begin to understand in this short small talk conversation you are having.

The year is 2017, Trump has just come into office. It's the end of February. We have only just started dealing with the racist depths that are his Presidency. I've gotten asked this question before, but it's the timing of it all, the political climate. My off-white, brown skin tone poking through at the corners of my eyes, the creases of my mouth, the color of my hair. It all gives away as just enough exotic, different, non-conforming, non-white, mullato... I don't know what this Brown cashier saw in me that day. But, he saw just enough of me to call me out, to put my non-whiteness on display.

Or maybe he just wanted to compliment me. "Your exotic Latina flavor adds a certain spice that I have been needing in my life, Miss." Or not. Maybe he just wanted to categorize me. "Ah-ha! A Mexican-American! I knew she wasn't white!" or "Ah-ha! An American-Mexican, I knew she was mixed!" Colored folks can be racists too, lest ye forget.

So when someone, a stranger, asks me what could be seen as a simple question to some, "What's your ethnicity?" It is actually a loaded question that I have to bottle up, so I don't explode at this innocent person, not meaning to stir up a lifetime of ancestral indigenous and colonial confusion.

If I weren't a citizen, or if I didn't feel safe saying where I was from this could be seen as a veiled threat. I know some people won't understand that. But I think of my family, coming over from Mexico. And now, I think of that checkout person at the grocery store, trying to make casual conversation with my aunt by asking her what ethnicity she is, and I see fear in her eyes. I see the questions she is asking herself, the risk assessment she is making in her mind. "Why is he asking me that? Who wants to know? Should I smile and pretend like I don't speak English? Where is he from? He's Brown too, but what kind of Brown? Is his Brown like my Brown? Or is he just some kid who doesn't know what he is asking?"

I'm a beautiful young woman, and when people ask me my ethnicity, more often than not, it is men asking me. I feel fetishized. In my mind they are dressing me up in a fruit hat, like Carmen Miranda, the Chiquita Banana lady, and I'm doing some exotic dance from another country that they just can't wait for me to teach them. I want to scream out, "that is none of your fucking business!" What will my ethnicity truly tell you, a stranger, about me? There are so many other things I could tell you about myself. Frankly, it doesn't matter what color my skin is in determining who I am, and as I'm a complete stranger to you, why don't you ask me my name?

Breath

This is the only ode I've ever written

Celia Nimura-Parmenter

Ode to you and our inside jokes

Ode to the alter egos we made for one another and ode to the time we spend

Ode to your smile that lights up the room and ode to those wishes we made

You wouldn't tell me yours because then it wouldn't come true

So I wrote mine down and folded up it up like a love note, don't worry though I'll give it to you once it happens

Ode to sitting here waiting to hand you my folded-up wish

Ode to tipping a hat to each other like an 18th century business man and I bow regally but

Instead of bowing back you decide to fall over laughing so I do the same

Letting myself fall into an imaginary field of flowers

Staring up at imaginary stars and planets

And from six feet apart the only thing I love more than falling is you catching me

Untitled

chanel athena e.

and lik e
                street gardens

        w e grew
                        intertwined w i t h
            chain-link
            fences.

shame.

Saiyare Refaei

I withstand another sit up and wonder who taught my women shame
Ex-lover raves over waxing sheets as aging heads recede
Mom pinches each hip bone like baby's cheeks
Auntie's ivory skin powdered with sugar and bleached with cream

Ex-lover raves over waxing sheets as aging heads recede
The labors of pain in the name of beauty
Auntie's ivory skin powdered with sugar and bleached with cream
Each morning before breakfast granny threads her eyebrows thin

The labors of pain in the name of beauty
Mom pinches each hip bone like baby's cheeks
Each morning before breakfast granny threads her eyebrows thin
I withstand another sit up and wonder who taught my women shame

Untitled

Tina Văn

If desire is the root of suffering
What is the root of desire?
It is
        Knowing the possibilities
And
        Feeling like I don't have to choose
In the end
I wish I'd have known
        Not choosing is a choice

Mixed Girls

Lauren Hoogkamer

Trace my skin:
White and black and brown—
Indescribable, I am all the colors in between.

Look in my eyes:
Slanted, big and small—
They're all the shapes of round.

Feel my hair:
It's curly, kinky, nappy
Sleek and straight and soft.

Kiss my lips:
Full and wide, small and thin.

Run your hands—
Down the sides of my pear-shaped,
Hourglass, will-o'-the-wisp hips.

I am tall and short, old and young
Beautiful in my own way.

Wrap me in your arms
Embrace the history
Of the seven continents of me.

Don't ask—
Don't let the details matter.
For now, just let it be me and you.

Perfect is my Utopian Sunset

Celia Nimura-Parmenter

The pigment only lasting for a moment before washing away with the sun

Unattainable and fleeting perfection impales me

I wonder how and why the orange and pink colors could fall away so quickly and easily

Shadows pointing distorted hands and throwing their heads back to laugh

I can't help but cower away from the shame and pointing fingers

The shadows fall slightly back, just enough for me to glance up and see that these are my shadows and underneath the darkened sky I'm standing on an ocean

My reflection is tainted with insecurity and I miss the utopian sunset of perfect, the comforting fantasy and mirage of confidence and joy

I look up my reflection and I see a crack in the wall of darkness and

We look closer and it's a star

We see another and another

Another three and then two more and suddenly there's thousands of them

We start to smile and then we start to love that smile

We start to love the fat on our thighs and the rolls on our stomach

Our hips dips and bags under our eyes
That weird thing we do when we get nervous and our illegible handwriting

Our short temper and high-pitched laugh that takes up a room and the fact that we cry during ten-minute Disney Shorts

All the imperfections and the things the shadows laughed at don't seem imperfect anymore they seem real.

We smile up at the shadows and in response they break farther and farther apart revealing acceptance and we no longer care about the shadows cast behind

Because finally, from the prison of the horizon

Our star breaks free

Dear Steve

Janae Hill

Dear Steve,

Let's talk. This relationship is not going to work.

You're sweet to me when I ignore what you do. And I must admit, we look great together when that happens.

But the moment I have to tame you, you unleash your fury.
You break poor, innocent, small combs.
You make my scalp a desert, nonexistent.
You greedily hold onto dead pieces forming twisted blobs of
monstrous hair balls. You brutally murder hair bands with your trashing.

I am terrified of dealing with you.
I'm unable to run my hands through you without you getting latched
onto my fingers.

But I can't keep letting you bully me.
I own you, not the other way around.
I'm stuck with you for life, so I will deal with you.
You are just hair. I will tame you.

Be ready, Steve. Your freedom is over.

Sincerely,

Janae.

Year of the Rat

Christina Vega

I. Considerations

You can stay at home and garden.
You can read.
You can write poems and letters.
You can have long, rambling phone conversations with people you haven't seen or touched in years.
You can admit it's the same as before, but different.
You can mend your clothes.
You can clean the kitchen like a good woman.
You can make the bed.
You can watch the birds until you cry and then keep crying because no one is looking.
You can check your bank account, again.
You can drink one cup of coffee per day.
You can regulate.
You can monitor your temperature.
You can monitor your fruit and meat and sugar intake.
You can input the number of hours you worked last week into a webform that will crash, again, but you can't get unemployment.

You can call the VA, again.
You can be addressed by most of your name, but not all of it.
You can be truncated, just like that.
You can adjust.
You can go almost a whole day without saying anything to the people in your house. You can call it your house, but it's not.
You can call the hotline, or your mom.
You can speak to the woman at WIC.
You can become a wraith, floating from room to room, silent.
You can accept some forms of public assistance without the floor falling out underneath you.
You can have nightmares.
You can imagine your stomach blossoming in the middle of the night and peeking in at your child. You'll know it's too early for her and it's too much.
You can wind yourself up real good.

You can be problematic.
You can check the "insured" box, but your claim will be denied.
You can get one pound of cheese, name brand if you want,

but you can't keep your dignity.
You can get canned or dried beans. It's your choice.
Your paperwork can get reevaluated, again, but never approved.
You can get peanut butter.
You can hear a heartbeat.
You can call and call and call and never get through.
You can feel shame enveloping you like a wave of warm water.
You can put the debit card down, there's no money.
You can get zero or one percent milk, even lactose free.
You can have a meltdown before and after you shower.
You can keep reading books about compost and decay.
You can panic before a video call and hang up when they answer.
You can bury your phone.

You can cook all your meals in cast-iron.
You can go to work twice a week.
You can pet the cat, but it won't pet you back.
You can write it out.
You can share zero of these poems with zero people.
You can reach your hand out looking for comfort.
You can lean in for a kiss and find a wall, instead.
You can press your face to the wall, anyway.
You can waste hours each day practicing foreign language vocabulary
sets you won't use.
"It's time to party." "Let's mingle." "What festival is it tomorrow?"
You can spend all morning reading Mary Ruefle. She will make you feel
better. Jim Harrison won't.
Jim Harrison will tell you about dead deer and you will be reminded
that you can wallow in city parks in gulches in distress where no one can
hear you. You can be a dead doe, rotting, having died in winter

now, staring out on this cruel luxuriance.

You can decide to live and speak exclusively in poems
only to find it's not safe there, either.
You can do it anyway.

You can quiet yourself down and rock yourself to sleep.

II. Decisions

Stay at home.
Close the door not your mouth.
Ask the mailman for a second, third and fourth key.
Stand on the porch in the dark and show your teeth.
Let them become a trap door.
Break the tree open and insert your tongue.
Run your hand through his hair kiss his neck.
Sequester inside another person's body.
Reorganize your closet.
Unlearn what you just learned so it won't hurt so bad.
Stare at the pineapple sage plant and rub its leaves
between your fingers like morning sex.
Don't say a word.
Don't disagree when someone sits at your table, drunk,
and talks to you about shame.
Don't tell them you didn't experience that kind.
Give them ice cream and wait it out.
Plant a garden.
Trample the neighbor's garden.
Dream of kittens and the Pleiades after Mary chastises you for being vague and
sentimental. You are both.
Lack specificity with vehemence then take it back.
Be vehement instead.
Play dominoes.
Avoid online workshops and open mics.
Avoid death.
Avoid department stores and hot tubs.
Avoid unwaxed floss.
Be unreasonable then apologize for starting the fight though you don't mean
it. Take your clothes off.
Run your hands along the new curves of your body.
Say good morning to them both.
Avoid your phone.
Avoid the violence of clothing with zippers.
Explain to another poet why parenthesis have no place in poems.
Tell them who taught you and hope they ask him, instead.
Burn the pancakes.
Burn the mail.

And whatever you do, don't get caught closing the windows and blinds.

New Year's Eve 2020

Lydia K. Valentine

They seem to think

> that when the ball drops and the bells peal,
> these layers of grime and greed,
> of gaslight and gunpowder,
> of grief and grievances

will peel

away.

Consequence can't be trammeled up so easily.

These four years are not the foundation of our country's faults.
Blood-washed sediment began to settle on these shores four hundred years
ago, and even more has

and **piled on,**
and **piled on,**
and **piled on,**

> every new year
> every new day

since.

Truck loads and handfuls of malice—

> sly, verbal micro-bullets at best
> state-sanctioned, viral murders at worst

—are dumped and thrown like ground-glass powder cast into the air.

We, of all castes, breathe this airborne malignance.
We, of all castes, are coated with it, inside and out.

Black life here has forever been a bloody business,
> our pain the perverse entertainment of
> picnic-lynchings
> phone-filmed lynchings
> souvenir postcards
> and social media posts.

So, no, the reign of this unprecedented poser-president was not the start,
but it and he legitimized and lithified these layers of toxicity.

What we need is a reckoning, a wrecking ball,
to reduce the white supremacist systems of this republic to dust,
to exhume and exalt our milled bones and our milled benevolence;

then, maybe, the be-all and end-all, the dream that could be America,
will be.

Bigfoot Plays Hide and Seek

Katherine Felts

I'm so fucking angry all the time.
Don't think it's a sign of anything bigger.
What kind of plant wouldn't wither
Under a stomping boot?
My point is moot, is dog whistled
Across a purple prairie free.
Life is a series of loss for me.
I'm in opposition to what should be
A heritage not yet stamped out.
Of course, it's not for lack of trying, and
When I attempt to be honest or loud
I'm accused of lying, you see:
Girls like me aren't to be believed.
We deceive everyone, cry wolf,
Cry other 4 letter words.
We're meant to be seen, not heard.
Better for everyone if we stay quiet.
Fed a steady diet of lying to myself.
Claiming that I'm healthy or fine or ok
Why can't I just say that I'm suffering
I knew it was grey here just not constantly
Maybe it's just me but it seems like a lot of people
With "adventure" blogs are kind of shitty
Perhaps I'm just jealous or bored or petty
Cause I'm scared of the outdoors
Scared of what's in store if I'm caught
Out when or where I shouldn't be
My fate being up to he or they or them
Not to me, remember control isn't welcomed
I dream of autonomy and peace
Nature too unreal a place for me
Any activity where I'm viewable is a problem
It doesn't feel like I can exist
And also solve it.

When the World Begins to End

Celia Nimura-Parmenter

It will start to rain around all the deer habitats in the forest

The deer's homes are flooded, and the wolves watch from the sun and laugh, proud of their sunny corners until a thunderstorm arrives

Lightning hits the wolves dens and all the deer laugh and say, "Well that's what they get for mocking us!!"

The wolves scare and shame the deer for laughing at them and the deer point at the lightning and say it's all the lightning's fault

To stop the lightning from inflicting apathy the wolves work to build a giant wall

The wolves will go to town meetings and boast about how wonderful the wall is

The wolves have the role of supposedly protecting deer by telling them what's best and the deer can't do anything

There will be a mass selling of shelters to protect from the lightning

Almost everyone will work making these shelters

If you're lucky you get to make rain boots or pretty umbrellas but if you do then people will laugh at you, "What are you, an intellectual? A struggling artist?"

When a lightning storm comes again everyone is better prepared

Deer don't get hit but one wolf's den does because of a broken shelter

Angered, the wolves set out to fire and shun to whoever made that broken shelter and unsurprisingly a deer is found guilty and shunned into exile as an example of what happens when we don't follow instructions properly

The wolves grow to live much better than the deer, cozy dens and safety from the rain while the deer struggle to find spots to sleep

But the wolves earned their comfort and safety, didn't they? And the deer deserved what they had for laughing at the wolves oh so long ago

Whenever the town chooses a leader all the voices of deer are silenced as punishment for mocking the wolves oh so long ago

Eventually the distance between wolves and deer will get bigger and the once dreaded thunderstorms will become normal

We won't have noticed that the deer are nearly all gone or that there are more thunderstorms than there used to be and if we did it wouldn't have mattered

The world will be used to the thunderstorms then and the few deer left tell us, "When the world begins to end, it will start to rain."

My Commitment to Us

Katherine Felts

I'm running into every cave screaming,
Bat swinging, singing songs of revolution!
Saying I'm tired.
Saying I tried finding other solutions.
I tried the other ways.
But I'm saying not today, motherfucker
We came to play, so buck up!
Y'all this isn't going to be fun or pretty
Rebuilding our country and cities
Takes hard work.
It'll be sweaty, and uncomfortable.
But we'll build the muscles we need
To propel ourselves forward
Toward futures built on equity and acceptance.
On the radical perspective that humanity and life
Should be respected.
That the collective is the only way to be.
It seems silly to some, and I know
It might be hard to believe in
Freedom
When all you've seen is pain,
But I think it's real strange how few of us
Are working to change
Into something different.
And don't have a mission.
And aren't trying to claim every god-given right.
And won't fight for what's theirs.
I know what it's like to be scared
And while it's not fair to not be included,
To be excluded from food, and from security
The fear in me can never outweigh my hope.
The power of *we* can't be understated.
So grab the rope and ascend, friend,
It was never fated for us
To bend to wills other than our own.

Sk'aliCh'elh-tenaut

Cervantes Gutierrez

"In the Lummi language, the term for killer whales is qwe 'lhol mechen, meaning 'our relations below the waves.' The Salish Sea Campaign is working to bring the orca Sk'aliCh'elh-tenaut out of captivity and back home to the Salish Sea"

> *– Salish Sea Campaign, continued by the Lummi-led non-profit, Sacred Lands Conservancy*

To our Relative beneath the sea,
She drummed and led the ceremony in the
water, These are the rights of nature
Your mother wants you home

She drummed and led the ceremony in the
water, When the sky turned all colors on my
tongue As if the sky people fell over in screams
Your mother wants you home

When the sky turned all colors in my tongue
Blooming new hopes in music
As if the sky people fell over in screams
Letting my wooden flute sing dangerous songs

Blooming new hopes in music
These are the rights of nature
Letting my wooden flute sing dangerous songs
To our relative beneath the sea.

Isn't that a call of love?

A Beggar's Lament

Lydia K. Valentine

If wishes were horses, I'd ride mine to the sun.
That truth bringer, that radiant mother,
watches me now   and waits.

If wishes were horses, I'd ride a fearsome mount
as big as forever, as loud as lost love.
The thundering Clydesdale would look up
at Her   in wonder.

If wishes were horses, I'd ride Make My Child Well.
She'd crunch two-ton blocks of tear-salt,
slurp down the wet fruit of my heart given freely,
take great gulps from a trench filled with blood
drained   from every vein.

If wishes were horses, I'd ride salvation to you.
I'd bathe your eyes and flush your ears in her mare's milk
to stop the visions and silence the voices escaped from the veil
that won't let you rest, that won't let you think,
that steal away your safety, your sense...
and you'd return to yourself, my love,   and you'd return to me.

You Should Know

Kellie Richardson

You should know
with you I find a particular kind of peace,
even as my skin crackles with their hate
despite loud, mocking shadows of the past.

When we are apart
I conjure you with a mind spell.
I pull and pluck and prune
for the gifts of memory and time.

When I'm out
on a limb
swirling and ducking
riding and catching

the waves,
you are with me,
keen to my unspoken wishes,
conscious to my queries.

Like starlings –
reverberating, murmuring.
Lock step, locked in,
tethered black to black to black.

Come to me
with fever bright
and fury blue –
We will feast and rest.

The old sandcastles
and trap doors disappear
because we no longer
participate in their existence.

When I enter the world
to earn my wage, build us a way,
they cut and kill me,
and each day I die,

bit by bit.
But my time here is sweeter
because I can summon you
from anywhere.

swimming for god
gloria joy kazuko muhammad

like gazing at an aquarium of fish

i stand in awe as the wind blows
their coverings that dance on their heads

i do not have a covering
that dances on my head

i seek to dance like them
but my heart only whispers

my heart does not know the dance
like they do

my spirit does not know the beat
like they do

i watch them form
in all shades of pashminas

verses dance
across collarbones

i only know coverings from bed sets
and those letters you attach for employment

my sepia face glistens, watching
their third eyes kiss the floor

every morning before the sun

these women are glass mirrors
that don't dare to break

majestic beings

that one cannot touch

they tell me majesty is

a covering of the heart
a diving of the spirit

entranced in oneness

i ask if oneness is available
for those whose hearts
are covered in rust
and sawdust

they exclaim to me, *yes!*

they lead me to the water
and my chest expands

spiritual surgery
has just begun

dune's day.

Saiyare Refaei

we climb this peak
 entering dune's day
celebrating all the grains
          of this earth
  that have withered away
          and raised us
          to these heights
     not knowing what winds
   will find us as we near the top
"living has become too precious a habit"
          not to forge another foot
          forward in sinking sand
     uncertainty brings out insecurity
               love is uplifting
     overpowering doubts in each muscle
          views may take you away
      when ill sentiments catch you
               out of breath
          for the youth's sake
       find hope in dreaming of
     the place you wish to create
          remember joy is liberation
    tend to your garden of loved ones
          with kindness and laughter
    further the growth of good medicine
               sing for your spirit
          let rays warm your heart
       let sea breezes calm your mind
       let shells tell you of a better time
                    for what we have to live
                    are these precious moments
                         together
                    we can never
                       recreate

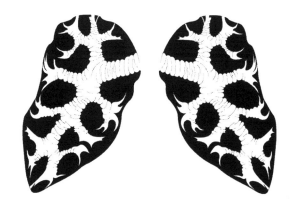

Contributor Bios

Kim Archer is a life-long artist who draws, entertains and holds crowds with her honest, soulful delivery. Whether she's playing a premier venue with her award-winning band, or an intimate solo show, she never disappoints! With guitar in hand, she commands the stage whether playing her own original songs or conjuring up a whole new vibe on a diverse set of your favorite covers. Known for her raw, powerhouse performances and unforgettable voice, her band has received multiple awards, and she is involved in various music projects.

Gaian Rena Bird is a Black Indigenous writer, poet, and artist living in Tacoma, WA. She is a self-defined sojourner crone who creates and writes from a place inseparable from the old ways of her ancestral roots in West Africa and Eastern Cherokee traditions. Having lived many lives from daughter to mother, from wild child to military wife, from victim to survivor, and church lady to Conjurer, her lived experience informs her writing and art with a deep love for herself and her people. This love is the heart of her journey. She says, "I write to know I am still breathing. I write to keep from sinking. I write because the world tells me no."

Phebe Brako-Owusu was born and raised in Ghana. She learned the importance of mental health and wellness when she started college in North Carolina. She is a trauma-trained licensed marriage and family therapist with a private practice based in Tacoma, WA. Phebe is passionate about serving People of Color and Immigrants. Her practice currently serves couples, families and individuals over the age of 13. Outside of work, Phebe spends her time being a mom to two boys, dancing in the aisles of retail spaces and loves trying new cooking recipes.

Aleyda Marisol Cervantes, or Mari for her familia, is a self-identified third world woman who grew up in a small town in Guadalajara, Mexico. She attended Western Washington University where she graduated from Fairhaven College with an Interdisciplinary major titled "Solidarity Across borders: Understanding Experiences and Imagining New Realities through Storytelling" and a minor in Education and Social Justice. She is a TEDx presenter and her research around transnational feminist literature has been presented in various conferences. She has been published in the anthology *Gendering Globalization, Globalizing Gender: Postcolonial Perspectives* Edited by Gül Çalışkan. She was also a Tin House workshop attendee and DreamYard Fellow 2020, a scholarship recipient for a scholarship for Frost Place Conference in 2020, and the international San Miguel de Writers Conference. She currently works at a community college building bridges between underrepresented students and the world of higher education and serves as a board member in Mujer al Volante, an organization cultivating leadership and autonomy for immigrant women. She also makes the time to write and dream a little more in occupied Coast Salish territory.

Judy Cuellar is a byproduct of the U.S. Army. The first born of Juan and Yong. Judy has been journaling for many years and while navigating the COVID pandemic had the privilege of participating in a few writing workshops. With the encouragement of her fellow workshop attendees, who are also talented and seasoned writers, she began to find additional depths of healing through writing. Judy hopes that her writing will be a conduit in which others will find their own version of comfort, joy, healing, and encouragement.

Paula Davidson is 26 years old. She's a Costa Rican Native. Libra. Earth Activists. Dreamer. Grower. Massage Therapist. Sustainability enthusiast. A lover of light. An experience of experiments. She walks on city streets.

Brandi D. Douglas is an Indigenous, Mexican, Black and queer-identifying femme who was born and raised in Tacoma, WA. She is a member of the Puyallup Tribe, and descendant of the Muckleshoot and Nooksack Tribes. Her pronouns are she/her/hers. She is a scholar, writer and entrepreneur, who owns The Multifaceted Matriarch, a digital decolonizing consulting company, and co-owns both American Indian Republic, a Native digital media company and Bella & Belle, a creative design studio. Additionally, she is a Board Member of the Tacoma Women of Color Collective and continually aspires to support the most vulnerable at the intersections of the PoC and LGBTQIA2S communities.

chanel athena estrada (they/siya > she) lives on Puyallup and Coast Salish lands. As a creative, they harness spiritual guides and ancestors forming poetry and capturing beauty found with(in) kapwa. Follow their journeys on instagram @uv.ube and @ultra.ube.

Katherine Felts is a Black/biracial poet who writes about how her intersecting identities affect her world, and how she witnesses it. Her work seeks to understand, and to demand attention for uncomfortable topics. She finds writing healing and hopes to teach writing workshops someday to help others find relief and freedom in using their voice.

Marissa Harrison is the author of her debut novel, *Rain City Lights*. As both an accountant and writer, she loves how stories are built with colorful details. She was born and raised in the Puget Sound, and writes psychological fiction that features strong, female protagonists, the rainy Pacific Northwest, social issues and crime. In her spare time Marissa enjoys running, hiking, dramatic miniseries and a great glass of wine. She lives in Seattle with her husband and four guinea pigs.

Jasmine Hernandez is a Spokane artist, poet, and mentor. She is currently studying Indigenous People's Law at the University of Oklahoma.

Janae Hill is a high school senior who loves to imagine worlds, write poetry and fiction, and read stories. She likes to play her cello and is trying to discover the world around her.

Lauren Hoogkamer is the Assistant Historic Preservation Officer for the City of Tacoma. She holds an MS in Historic Preservation and an MS in Urban Planning from Columbia University, as well as a BA/BA in Print Journalism and History and a Minor in Business from the University of Southern California. She has received awards for journalism and poetry and has research published by the World Monuments Fund. Lauren grew up in rural Lewis County, WA, but now lives in Tacoma with her husband, two sons, a dog, and a cat. As a historic preservation professional, she wants to ensure that our built environment represents and meets the needs of our diverse community. Her writing is inspired by her experiences as a multicultural woman; she is Mexican, Trinidadian, Black, French, Chinese, East Indian, and a little bit of almost everything else.

Isha Hussein is a young, Black, and Muslim activist from Tacoma, WA. She has presented at the Race and Pedagogy National Conference hosted by the University of Puget Sound, has been featured in The New Yorker in an article entitled "The Perils of People of Color" and is actively involved with The People's Assembly as a community organizer. Isha is the Commission Chair for the Justice & Safety Division of the Tacoma Mayor's Youth Council. Her poetic artwork, "To All My Opposites," was featured at Alma Mater's Milk Gallery in an exhibit entitled, "Abolition: Imagining How We Get Free." She sees writing as a way to express herself and hopes that when people read her words, they feel connected and have a way to positively escape. Isha desires to be a politician and a role model that fights for people no matter what (including the homeless population, minorities, and those without food). Contact Isha by email at ishaaahussein@gmail.com.

Eileen Jimenez's mother is Maria Cruz Jimenez, her grandmother is Eloisa Saavedra and her great grandmother is Isidora Saavedra, matriarchs of the Otomi people. She is an indigenous queer artist. Her soul speaks through her art and writing, in it, she sees herself and the stories and the strength from her ancestors. As a indigenous leader, community member, and as an artist, everything she does and creates is influenced by her many intersecting identities and lived experiences. She creates the art, the structures, the programming and the educational experiences she wishes her community and she would have seen and had access to as a girl from the 'hood.' Her family's stories, values, theories and practices keep her feeling whole throughout this process and she finds support through community care.

Kathleen Julca founded Chicas of Technology to provide a supportive environment for cohorts of girls to receive computing education and mentorship. She conducts research about driving factors and solutions for women's disparity in computer science and leads technology education initiatives through the Coding Club she founded and through the Civil Air Patrol. There, she is technical sergeant and her Cyber Patriot team placed first in state for the all-service division. She studied Mobile App Development at MIT's Online Science Technology and Engineering Course, Design Connect Create Physics at Rice University, and robotics through John's Hopkins University. She enjoys exploring physics through projects such as creating a cloud chamber and serving as an intern at Pierce College's plasma ray project. She was a national winner of the NCWIT's Aspirations in Computing and helped create the Congressional-App-Challenge Winner: Women of Color Code. She plans on studying Computation and Cognition at her undergraduate institution.

Marisha McDowell was born in India and adopted to have a chance at a better life in America. She grew up in Tacoma, Washington and has resided in Olympia, Washington for over ten years. She identifies with she/her pronouns, is a champion for all underdogs, and is a trauma informed social worker. She is a feminist, brown-skinned and forever working to remember to not let my voice be quieted in this loud world. She writes for meaning, sanity and to save her own soul by sharing her truth.

Stasha Moreno is a Tacoma native. She received her bachelors in Creative Writing from Bard College. She is proudly Mexican American and a second generation immigrant.

Gloria Joy Kazuko Muhammad is a literary arts teaching artist, educator, and writer based in Puyallup Tribe territory (Tacoma, WA). Gloria leads with compassion and has a heart for community building. As a writer, Gloria is inspired by spirituality, everyday life, nature, music, and cinematography. She is a graduate of Washington State Teaching Artist Training Lab and is excited to host writing workshops rooted in healing and personal development. Find Gloria on Instagram @whoisgloriajoy, by email at gloriajoymuhammad@gmail.com, or at sites.google.com/view/whoisglo-riajoy.

Celia Nimura-Parmenter is a proud biracial queer 15-year-old currently attending Tacoma School of The Arts. She is an unofficial costumer and seamstress selling clothes at Sumiko Vintage (@sumikovintage on Instagram), a performing artist and a poet.

Krista Perez, founder and president of TWCC, has spent the bulk of her education and career learning and prioritizing anti-racist, equitable and community centered work. Her multi-disciplinary perspective allows her to view her work through several lenses which include being the daughter of an immigrant father and migrant worker mother, her undergraduate degree in law, economics and public policy, small business/entrepreneurial knowledge, and passion for community organizing. These experiences inform the work that Krista has done through this nonprofit organization, her PoC centered market, The Community Market, and her equity consulting business, Perez Consulting.

Lev Pouliot is a non-binary, non-monogamous, mixed-race chaotic Libra. Punk-adjacent and determinedly leftist, they are a Midwest native and came to Tacoma by way of the South, and currently live between Central and Hilltop as a PolyRev house gremlin. They spend most of their time writing, collaging, brooding and breaking curses.

Saiyare Refaei (they/them/she/her) is a Chinese-Iranian artist and community organizer currently occupying traditional lands of the Puyallup Tribe of Indians also known as Tacoma, WA. Their mediums mostly include community murals, printmaking, and meticulous pointillism drawings, mostly. Saiyare strives to utilize art and writing as a means of community building, education, and healing. They enjoy working collaboratively and being a conduit to visualize the stories that need to be told in our communities. This is Saiyare's first poetry publication. You can follow Saiyare's journey on Instagram at @_saikick_ and on the Justseeds Artists' Cooperative website, justseeds.org.

Kellie Richardson is a writer, artist and educator born and raised in Tacoma, Washington. Kellie believes her work has one purpose: to be used as a tool for liberation and healing. Sometimes through provocation or confession, other times through belly laughs or tears, Kellie works to center the beauty and power of everyday folk and put some funk into the dread we call survival. She served as the Poet Laureate of Tacoma from 2017 – 2019, working to hold and curate spaces that centered Black, Brown, and LGBTQ voices. Kellie drinks and thinks too much, doing her best work under a blanket. In addition to writing, Kellie is a mixed media artist, lecturer, and hip-hop head.

Katharine Threat is a mixed-race writer from the D.C. area who focuses her writing on the subjects of race, identity, and the concept of home. She graduated from the University of Puget Sound with a BA in Art History and English Creative Writing, and is passionate about generating and maintaining safe and encouraging spaces for young artists to express themselves and share their art. She wants to work with contemporary artists of all media and foster sympathetic, earnest, and socially active communities through art.

Kaia Valentine is a poet and short story author from Tacoma, Washington. She has a bachelors degree in political science and philosophy, which culminated in a successful thesis on the modern phenomenon of transracialism. She values spirituality, intersectionality, emotional intelligence, anti-colonialism, and deep dissections of American culture. Her greatest joys in life are family, her wonderful pets, her superbly supportive girlfriend, Heather, literature, music, and the power that stems from trained critical thinking.

Lydia K. Valentine is a playwright and poet, director and dramaturg, editor and educator. Her proudest accomplishment, though, is being a mom to two creative, intelligent, and caring individuals and activists. In her own writing and the projects to which she contributes through Lyderary Ink, Lydia seeks to amplify the voices of those who are often stifled, ignored, and marginalized in what has been the accepted narrative of the United States. Lydia's first poetry collection, *Brief Black Candles*, was published in November 2020 by Not a Pipe Publishing.

Tina Văn (they/them, she/her) is a nonbinary femme who is awakening from a dualistic world. They were born into a family of Vietnamese immigrants and hail from Hilltop, Tacoma, where they are exploring the layers of their displaced identity. Tina enjoys singing, dancing, reading, and writing. Find Tina on Instagram @tinathevan.

Christina Vega is a Queer Chicana poet. They're also a veteran from New Mexico with a passion for storytelling and community involvement. They're the publisher at Blue Cactus Press and a teaching artist with Write253. They live and write in Tacoma, Washington, with their family but dream of returning to the desert one day to write in an adobe house. Christina's debut poetry collection, *Still Clutching Maps,* was published in 2017. Follow Christina on Twitter @bluecactuspress and Instagram @ccthemighty.

Jesi Hanley Vega is a native of The Bronx and a transplanted Tacoman. A former screenwriter and documentary filmmaker, Jesi now finds joy as a book editor, writing instructor, and communications consultant. When not working, Jesi loves writing fiction, practicing guitar, and bouncing on her mini-trampoline. She's also a fantastic cook. Jesi is the mom of two and the stepmom of two more, and is deeply grateful for her loving partner, Marc.

Jami Williams is a 23-year-old queer, Afro-Latinx and Indigenous woman. She's from Tacoma, WA and graduated from UW-Tacoma with her BA in Ethnic, Gender, and Labor studies. Her poetry is very personal to her, but she always writes in hopes that it is inviting or relatable and that others may see themselves in what she writes, too.

may you be,

carried, like wind
grounded, like soil
nourished, like water
reminded, like sky

for we are with you,
like breath

thank you for considering
choosing
listening

thank
you

for

being.

grateful to bear witness,

gloria joy kazuko muhammad,
editor, We Need A Reckoning

Hello, Dear Reader,

Here you are, at the back of the book, having (hopefully) read this beautiful anthology from cover to cover, a journey worth repeating again and again, a cycle of wind, soil, water, sky, and breath. Here, in the quiet pause between cycles, I'd like to offer heartfelt thanks to everyone who brought this book to life, including you.

This anthology would not have been possible without the monumental community support of readers, writers, and friends of the press who've watched it grow over the last five years; the emotional and technical support of badass women and femmes of color who worked on the design, editorial, and marketing components; and the generous financial support of the Tacoma Arts Commission. Without each one of our conspirators, this collection would not exist. Thank you, as well, to the Tacoma Women of Color Collective and the incredible women under its umbrella for supporting this anthology and what it stands for. It is an offering to – and for – us. Our stories matter.

Lastly, I'm asking you, reader, to continue the work of uplifting the voices and stories of women and femmes of color within our community and the publishing industry, at large. This means celebrating and sharing our work publicly, hiring us in your practices, buying our books, listening to our stories, acknowledging our expertise, and standing by us in true friendship and solidarity. This is the work. And there is so much work to do before the professional landscapes we walk through reflect the breadth and diversity of our lived experiences.

Now, let's begin the cycle again,

Christina Vega
Publisher | Blue Cactus Press